learning to cook with natural foods

delia quigley   polly pitchford

The Book Publishing Company

dedication

This cookbook is dedicated to our parents, Hugh and Mary Ann Quigley and Louise and Stewart Hynd, whose love and support have been our foundation.

Special thanks to Susan Christy and Mort Chalfy for their encouragement and friendship and to David Routenberg, the best produce man in Florida.

**authors: delia quigley
polly pitchford**

art and design: eleanor dale evans

photography: thomas johns

food stylist: louise hagler

ISBN 0-913990-55-8 LCC- 87-33007

Quigley, Delia
   Starting over : learning to cook with natural foods / by Delia Quigley and Polly Pitchford
p.   cm.

        Includes index.
        ISBN 0-913990-55-8 :
        1. Cookery (Natural foods)   I. Pitchford, Polly.   II. Title.
        TX741.Q54 1988
        641.5'637—dc19   87-33007
                                                                    CIP

2 3 4 5 6 7 8 9 0

contents

introduction

preface 4
making the transition 4
menu planning 6
the natural foods pantry 8
glossary of unusual ingredients 10
macrobiotics 12
preparation tips

    grains 13
    beans 13
    sweeteners 14
    nuts 15
    tofu 15
    soup stock 15
    sprouts 16

cooking terms explained 17
before you begin 18

recipes

breakfast, breads & sandwiches 19
appetizers 33
salads 39
soups 49
sauces 57
side dishes 65
main dishes 76
desserts 110
beverages 136

appendix

appendix 138
    measures & equivalents
    nutritional analyses

index 139

about the authors 143

preface

My enthusiasm for food was matched in 1984 when I met Polly across a natural foods deli chopping block. We found that we had in common the basic staffs of life: a love for good vegetarian food and an outrageous sense of humor. Both with our Fine Arts degrees in Theater and an urge to do something "more" we soon combined our cooking and performing skills and in 1985 the first television production of "The Granary Gourmet" was aired in Sarasota, Florida.

This book is a collection of the recipes taken from a year and a half of our television show. The wide variety of foods and concoctions in this cookbook were born out of weekly inspirations ranging from a song, to a holiday season, to a craving, to a customers request etc. The result is a collection of delicious recipes to suit any food mood that you're in. We hope you enjoy them as much as we have enjoyed creating them.

Delia Quigley

making the transition

In an era of superior technologies, heightened intelligence, and sophisticated arts and sciences, one would think that mankind could do away with war, starvation and degenerative diseases. Yet the fighting continues, millions of people starve to death and the five most deadly diseases continue unchecked. Cancer, heart disease, obesity, arteriosclerosis and high blood pressure kill millions of people each year and research shows that improper diet is a major contributor.

Isn't it time you educated yourself as to what is best for your body and what you can do about preventing disease for yourself and your loved ones?

When I became a vegetarian in 1971 there was very little written information or recipes available. Learning to cook was an experimental process that required creativity in cooking outside the "Four Basic Food Group" guidelines of the Standard American Diet. I was raised on meat and potatoes. Sundays my mother would bake a chicken and Fridays were for fish fry dinners. There were always a lot of hamburgers and ham sandwiches on white bread, just like the standard American diet. Unfortunately, vegetables consisted of a small side salad or overcooked canned and frozen varieties, nothing that would excite a child's palate.

Today my diet includes fresh fruits and vegetables every day. When I decided to forego eating beef and pork I still had no inkling as to what part natural carbohydrates could play in my diet. Eliminating meat was the first step in my diet transition. I continued to eat chicken and fish as I began to experiment with brown rice and steamed vegetables. Simple and easy to do, I would layer the veggies over the rice and top with grated cheese.

Step by step I began to read and learn more about the foods I was eating and how they could affect my body. I discovered it to be an enjoyable and surprisingly easy challenge and one that opened up a whole new world of tastes and appreciation for natural foods preparation. The transition was easy when I eliminated one food at a time and substituted its healthier, more natural counterpart. Refined flour and bakery products were replaced by whole wheat breads and rolls. Table salt was exchanged for sea salt, tamari, soy sauce and in most cases just herbs and spices. I used sea vegetables for my calcium intake and bean-grain combinations for sufficient protein. Morning coffee became herb tea or a hot grain beverage. The hardest of all, sugar, was replaced with honey, maple syrup and fruit juices.

It has taken 15 years to complete my food transition but I feel healthier, younger and better than I ever have in my life. You can also as you change your diet step by step. A few changes will be required on your part but making a slow transition will make it a lot easier for the body, and soon you'll find that there's a whole new world of delicious tastes in natural foods. You will experience renewed energy and feelings of well being as you change your diet.

This book is an excellent starting point for your first step towards changing old eating habits. We have developed these recipes with the beginner in mind for simple, easy preparation. Use the spaces provided to alter recipes, make notes on new ideas, or document your dietary changes. This is your workbook. Use it in good health and it will open a whole new world of cooking and eating for you. Enjoy and Bon Appetit!

notes

menu planning

One of the biggest decisions you face as a prospective vegetarian is what to do with the hole left on your dinner plate once you eliminate meat, chicken or fish from the menu. Fortunately the market place has responded with a variety of new products that emulate meat and poultry in taste and texture. These meat substitutes appear as "hot dogs", burgers, sausage links, stew chunks and even frozen imitation "chicken breasts". These products have a useful place in the transition to vegetarianism. They're a source of quick-to-fix meals and can substitute for a meat item in your old stand-by recipes. Use these products sparingly, however, as they're processed foods, containing additives and preservatives.

Vegetarian products like tofu, tempeh and low-fat dairy products can easily fill the void in meal planning. They can be adapted to fit into favorite recipes, such as barbeque, pasta dishes, stews, casseroles and in some cases even desserts. Because of the high fat content in cheese, we recommend that you not rely on it as your main source of protein, but use to accent or complement your meals.

Vegetarianism offers some exciting adventures in eating. Only in America are meals highly structured around meat, with vegetables coming in a distant third after dessert. Ethnic cuisine offers a wide variety of alternatives to meat and potatoes. Mexican cooking uses pinto beans; Middle Eastern recipes, garbanzo beans; Far Eastern dishes use tofu and tempeh; Italian recipes call for pasta and cheese. Menus need not rely on any one dish to be the star attraction. A salad, casserole and bread can work together to provide a balance of color, texture and flavors that will make the meal a pleasure.

Protein is one of the main nutritional concerns for a vegetarian. The meat that has been eliminated from the diet was a primary source of protein. The current "recommended daily dietary allowance" for protein now stands at 56 grams for a man and 44 grams for a woman.[1] Variances on this standard depend on your build, level of stress and activity in your lifestyle and your general health. By adding up the amount of protein per serving listed under any of the recipes in this book you can get an idea of how to mix and match dishes to give you the protein you need. A little practice and your own experience will soon make this process easy and you'll get a feel for how much is enough without a lot of arithmetic. Two good sources for more information on this are the books **Diet for a Small Planet** and **The New Laurel's Kitchen**.

[1]Food and Nutrition Board, National Academy of Sciences, National Research Council, Recommended Dietary Allowances, 9th ed. Washington, D.C.: p.46, 1980

The additional vegetables and fruits used in a vegetarian diet usually contribute enough vitamins, minerals and carbohydrates that it's easy to get adequate amounts of these nutrients. If a vegetarian chooses not to use any dairy products, they will need to supplement vitamin B12.

Here are suggestions for how you can combine some of the recipes in this book to make delicious meals.

BRUNCH
Tea Muffins, pg.24,
Drop Biscuits, pg. 24
Dried Fruit Jam, pg. 64
Tofu Nut Puree, pg.37
Grilled Tofu, pg. 78
Maple Nut Millet, pg. 20
Fruit Soup, pg. 51
Granola Deluxe, pg.20

LUNCH
Cool Avocado Soup, pg. 50
Rainbow Pasta Salad, pg. 48
Bean Tostada, pg. 31
Maple-Almond Cookies, pg. 123

DINNER DATE
Vegetable Pate, pg. 36
Spicy Tomato Peanut Soup, pg. 54
California Salad, pg. 47
Pasta Primavera, pg. 109
Glazed Pears, pg. 131

SUMMER DINING
Hummus, pg. 34
Zucchini Yogurt Soup, pg. 50
Mixed Grain Salad with Yogurt
    Dressing, pg. 43
Cardamom Carrots, pg. 66
Lemon Mousse, pg. 129

PICNIC
Sloppy Joes, pg. 89
Sunflower Potato Salad, pg. 41
Baked Beans, pg. 94
Gran American Apple Pie, pg. 118

MACROBIOTIC MEAL
Miso-Wakame Soup, pg. 52,
Stuffed Cabbage Rolls with
    Butternut Sauce, pg. 106
Daikon Slaw, pg. 40
Roasted Almond Cookies, pg. 128

INDIAN FEAST
Curried Split Pea Soup, pg. 51
Curried Tempeh Wrap, pg. 92
Fruit and Mango Chutnies, pg.63,
Raita, pg. 132

DIET MEAL
Tofu Dip with raw
    vegetables pg. 35
Humble Miso Soup, pg. 52
Sprout Salad with Miso
    Dressing, pg. 40
Mushroom Tofu Stroganoff, pg. 79
Carob-Yogurt Cheesecake, pg. 117

HOLIDAY DINING
Tempeh-Almond Pate, pg. 36, Garlic-Dill Cheese Dip, pg. 34, Carrot-Yogurt Soup, pg. 56, Mock Turkey en Croute, pg. 88, Cornbread Stuffing, pg. 72, Braised Chestnuts and Brussel Sprouts, pg. 66, Stuffed Butternut Squash, pg. 67, Cranberry-Orange Nut Bread, pg. 25, with Orange Sesame Sauce, pg. 60, Creamy Pumpkin Pie, pg. 120

the whole foods pantry

Here is a list of foods and ingredients that we use most often in our recipes. If you are just starting to cook with whole foods it's a good idea to stock up on just a few items at a time. You can add more to your shelf as you go until you have a well stocked pantry from which you can create a huge variety of wonderful dishes. A glossary of some unfamiliar ingredients follows these pages.

beans

Adzuki Beans
Garbanzos (Chick Peas)
Pinto Beans
Black Beans

nuts & seeds

Sesame Seeds
Almonds
Cashews
Walnuts
Sunflower Seeds

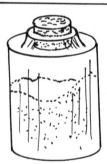

grains, cereals & breads

Brown Rice
Millet
Barley
Cous-Cous
Bulghar Wheat

Rolled Oats
Corn Meal
Whole Wheat Chapatis
Corn Tortillas

oils

Safflower
Sesame
Toasted Sesame
Corn
Olive

flours

Whole Wheat
Whole Wheat Pastry
Rice
Rye

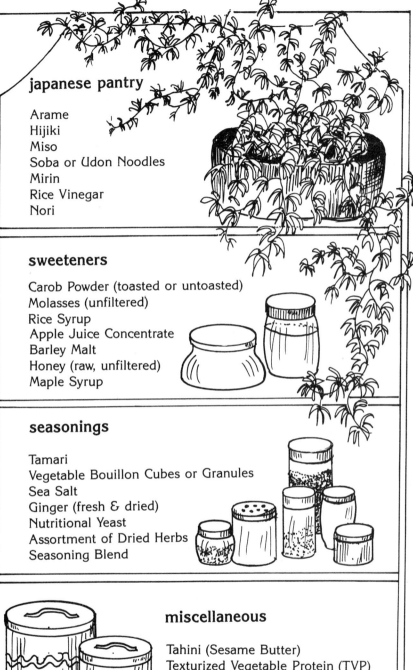

japanese pantry

Arame
Hijiki
Miso
Soba or Udon Noodles
Mirin
Rice Vinegar
Nori

sweeteners

Carob Powder (toasted or untoasted)
Molasses (unfiltered)
Rice Syrup
Apple Juice Concentrate
Barley Malt
Honey (raw, unfiltered)
Maple Syrup

seasonings

Tamari
Vegetable Bouillon Cubes or Granules
Sea Salt
Ginger (fresh & dried)
Nutritional Yeast
Assortment of Dried Herbs
Seasoning Blend

miscellaneous

Tahini (Sesame Butter)
Texturized Vegetable Protein (TVP)
Arrowroot
Assorted Dried Fruits

glossary of unusual ingredients

agar-agar   A flavorless sea vegetable used like gelatin to make molded salads and desserts. Agar-agar comes in flake, powder or stick form.

arame   See sea vegetables.

arrowroot   A natural thickener made from the arrowroot plant. It is most commonly used for sauces and should be dissolved in a small amount of cooking liquid before being added back to the pan to avoid lumping.

carob   Made from the pods of the carob tree, carob is a good substitute for chocolate. It is high in minerals, low in fat and naturally sweet so less sweeteners are needed in baking. Carob is available toasted or untoasted, in powder or block form.

daikon   This is a Japanese white radish, good for cutting fat and mucus deposits in the body. Grated daikon is used to help digest oily foods.

gomazio   A sesame seed seasoning made from seeds that have been toasted and ground. Gomazio is a wonderful alternative to salt. If desired, one part sea salt can be combined with four parts sesame seeds.

kombu   See sea vegetables.

mirin   A traditional Japanese seasoning and natural sweetener, mirin is made from sweet rice, rice koji (a cultured rice) and spring water. Use a dash for marinades, salad dressings, noodle broths or to mellow out salty or overly spicy foods.

miso   A paste made from soy beans, barley, water, sea salt and koji (a cultured rice mold). Miso aids in digestion and assimilation of other foods. It is most commonly used to flavor soups, sauces and spreads.

mochi   A solid rice cake made from cooked, pounded sweet rice. When baked it puffs and becomes crisp. It can be grated and melted as a topping instead of cheese.

muesli cereal   A traditional European breakfast cereal made of whole grains and sweetened only with dried fruits. It usually contains: rolled oats, rye, corn flakes, raisins, etc.

nori   A seaweed in flat sheets, usually pretoasted.

nutritional yeast   A food yeast (saccharomyces cerevisiae) grown on a molasses base that contains all the essential amino acids, is a good source of protein and B-vitamins, comes in yellow flakes or powder form and tastes good.

sea salt   This is sun-dried and unrefined and contains trace minerals removed in processed salt.

seasoning mix   Any one of the seasoning products on the market today. Be sure to read the ingredients and check that salt isn't one of the main ingredients. Beware of sugar in these, too.

sea vegetables   These plants need to be introduced into every household because they are a superior source of vitamins and minerals. Arame is a good one to start with because of its mild flavor. Some sea vegetables need to be soaked, others roasted and crumbled on salads and vegetables. Some need to be cooked just like ordinary 'land' vegetables. Be sure to do some reading of your own on these sea greens and see what they can offer you.

shitake mushroom   A large medicinal dried mushroom from Japan, called 'The Cadillac of mushrooms'

tahini   A nut butter made from ground sesame seeds. Tahini is a very good source of calcium and protein.

tamari   Tamari is a Japanese soy sauce. We recommend it over other soy sauces because it is naturally aged for two years in wooden kegs and has a richer, less salty taste. Tamari is also available in "wheat-free" and "low-sodium" varieties. Excellent with soups and grains. Substitute 2 to 3 parts tamari for 1 part salt.

tempeh   Tempeh, like tofu, is a soybean product. It has been eaten for centuries in Indonesia but is new to the West. It is made by a process of fermentation of the split soy beans. High in protein and a good source of B12, tempeh is more flavorful than tofu but still mild tasting and has an appealing, chewy texture. It should be steamed for at least 10 minutes before using.

tofu   Known in the Orient as 'The meat with no bones' because of its high protein content. It is soybean curd made from soymilk (which is made from soybeans). It's high in protein, low in calories and carbohydrates and contains no cholesterol. For more information, see page 15.

triticale   A grain whose flavor and cooking properties are a cross between wheat and rye.

tvp   A dry precooked food made from soybeans. The granules are hydrated into chewy chunks in hot water and add protein, vitamins and minerals to a dish.

wakame   A mild tasting sea vegetable that is often used in soups.

wehani rice   A newly bred grain grown in California. Its kernel is longer than brown rice, rust in color and has a nuttier taste.

macrobiotics

Many descriptions have been given this special way of living one's life. Concerning diet, it is a philosophy of eating that involves the use of organic and seasonal foods grown in your own environment. Whole grains, fresh vegetables, cooked fruits, beans, soy products and fermented foods are emphasized.

Macro (meaning large or long) and biotic (meaning life) was first brought to the United States from Japan in the late fifties by George Ohsawa. He translated the term Macrobiotics to mean "the art of longevity". Based on what he terms the "Unique Principle of Yin and Yang", or the relationship of opposites, Ohsawa describes his theory as two fundamental and opposite factors that continually produce and destroy everything that exists. He claims that all phenomenon and the character of all things are influenced by these two fundamental forces: the centripetal, "contractive" yang and the centrifugal "expansive" yin.

All foods are classified relative to substances that are extremely yin, such as sugar, drugs and fruits, or extremely yang, like meat, eggs or salt. The more moderate foods are beans, vegetables and sea vegetables, the most balanced of all being whole grains. For each individual to create a healthy way of eating the balancing of yin and yang is most important.

Today Ohsawa's main disciples, Michio Kushi and Herman Aihara, continue to teach this philosophy gaining more and more support from people seeking an effective healing lifestyle.

We find it to be a very valuable way of life and recommend that you explore the subject further on your own. You will find a number of recipes in this book that qualify as macrobiotic. These recipes are marked with the yin/ yang symbol:

preparation tips

cooking grains:

grain (1 cup dry)	water	cooking time	yield
Brown Rice	2 cups	40 minutes	3 cups
Wild Rice	3 cups	1 hour or more	4 cups
Barley	3 cups	1¼ hours	3½ cups
Buckwheat (Kasha)	2 cups	15 minutes	2½ cups
Millet	3 cups	25 minutes	3½ cups
Whole Wheat Berries	3 cups	2 hours	2½ cups

The first step in preparing whole grains is to rinse them thoroughly. They have been stored in dusty grain bins before ending up in your kitchen so they need to be rinsed until the water runs clear. The following chart lists the approximate amount of water per 1 cup of grain. Bring to a boil, cover with a tight fitting lid and reduce heat to low and simmer for the remainder of the cooking time. We like to turn off the heat just before the grain is done and allow it to steam the remainder of the time. This method prevents scorching accidents and makes for a fluffier grain.

cooking beans:

bean (1 cup soaked)	water	cooking time simmer/pressure cook*	yield
Black Beans	4 cups	1½ hours/30-35 min.	2 cups
Garbanzos (Chick Peas)	4 cups	2 hours/30-40 min.	2 cups
Kidney Beans	3 cups	1½ hours/25-30 min.	2 cups
Pinto Beans	3 cups	2 hours/30-40 min.	2 cups
Navy Beans	2 cups	1½ hours/15-20 min.	2 cups
Soy Beans	3 cups	pressure cook only/ 45 min.-1 hour	2 cups
Adzuki Beans	4 cups	2 hours/8 min.	2 cups
Lentils & Split Peas	3 cups	simmer only for 1 hour	2¼ cups

*at 15 lbs. pressure

Cooking times are approximate.

As with grains, beans need to be washed and sorted through before cooking. Equally important, beans should be soaked overnight or for several hours before cooking for two reasons: first, cooking time is reduced by a good half hour or more; second, beans are easier to digest when pre-soaked. Pour off the soak water and add at least 3 times the amount of cooking water as there are beans, add a bay leaf and some powdered ginger (or a piece of Kombu seaweed) to eliminate the 'gassy' qualities. Bring the water to a boil, reduce heat to medium and cook at a gentle boil until tender, adding more water if necessary. Keep the pot covered while cooking. Lentils and split peas require no soaking or par-boiling and will be tender in 45 minutes to 1 hour. Pressure cooking is recommended especially for soybeans and will greatly reduce cooking time for most beans.

To shorten cooking time if you don't soak the beans overnight, add the cooking water to the clean beans, cover, bring to a boil and boil for 2 minutes. Turn off the heat and let beans stand for 1 hour. Then add the bay leaf, bring to a boil, and cook until tender.

A meal with well cooked dried beans, lentils or split peas provides protein and significant amounts of vitamins and minerals. The protein is enhanced by serving the beans with a grain. Beans and grains are both cholesterol and fat-free and are an excellent source of fiber.

sweeteners

One of the biggest controversies in natural food circles is around the use of granulated sugar vs. honey. Proponents of honey claim it has greater nutritional value than sugar. Recent nutritional studies report that honey is actually a liquid form of sugar with minute amounts of B vitamins, Iron and phosphorus.* Some of our recipes are made with honey for the taste and sweetness it imparts. However, there are alternative sweeteners you might try that would be even healthier for you. Maple syrup, barley malt and rice syrups (known also as yinnie) are three sweeteners you could try instead of sugar or honey. Fruit juice or fruit juice concentrates (frozen varieties) are also good substitutes and give a mild sweetness and lightness to cakes or cookies.

As a rule when substituting one cup barley malt, maple syrup or fruit juice for sugar, decrease ¼ cup of liquid from the rest of the recipe. Remember, though, sweets are sweets in any form so use sparingly.

*Tufts University, Diet & Nutrition Newsletter, Vol. 5, No.11, Jan. 1988

toasting nuts and seeds

There are quite a few recipes in this book that call for toasted nuts and/or seeds because the improvement toasting makes on their flavor is well worth the effort. Besides, the methods are very simple.

Seeds: Place seeds in a dry frying pan over medium-high heat and continually move the pan back and forth over the heat as they cook to avoid burning. Some seeds begin to pop while they cook so watch your eyes. They are done cooking when they are evenly browned and their aroma fills the kitchen!

Nuts: Spread the desired amount of nuts on a cookie sheet or pie plate and bake in a preheated 350 degree oven for anywhere from 10 to 20 minutes depending upon the size and density of the nut.

tofu - care & handling

Tofu is sold in blocks in health food stores and packaged in some grocery stores. Try to buy the freshest blocks you can. You can store it in water in a plastic container and change water daily (it will keep up to a week). It can be frozen in the package, a good way to keep extra tofu that you can't use up while fresh. Once it has defrosted, press out the excess liquid. Frozen tofu has a chewy texture. A one pound block of tofu yields 2 cups crumbled.

vegetable stock

To me vegetable stock is not just about making a good soup base. It is also about using the scrap pieces of produce that can be wasted so easily. The stock I make is from carrot tops and end pieces, the peelings from scrubbed veggies as well as the core of cauliflower and cabbage. All the odds and ends that one usually just throws in the garbage or uses for compost can be saved over a three or four day period and then placed in a big stock pot, covered with water and cooked for up to an hour on simmer. (Bring to a boil first then reduce heat to simmer). When finished cooking, strain the liquid making sure to press the liquid from the cooked vegetables. Store the liquid in a jar with a cover and refrigerate until you use it. You can also freeze it for future use in soups or sauces. It will keep in the fridge for four or five days and by that time you'll have enough pieces to start another batch of stock.

sprouting

Growing your own sprouts is an easy and cost efficient way to have nutritious foods available year round. All that is needed is a glass jar, a small screen to cover the top and a rubber band to hold the screen in place. You can also purchase sprouting jars in your local health food store but they're not much different from what you can make yourself.

Use the following chart to get an idea of amounts and sprouting times for individual seeds. Small seeds such as alfalfa, radish, mustard, cabbage, cress etc., use 2 tablespoons for a 1 quart jar. Larger seeds such as wheat, mung, lentils, adzuki etc., use ½ cup for a 1 quart jar.

seeds	sprouting time	length of sprout
Alfalfa	3-4 days	1″
Soy	3 days	1/2″-3/4″
Mung	3-4 days	2″-3″
Wheat (soft)	2 days	same size as the grain
Lentils	2-3 days	same size as the lentil

how to sprout:

1. Place the seeds in a glass jar. Cover with water and let soak eight hours.

2. Cover the top of the jar with the screen and secure with the rubber band. Drain the water from the jar.

3. Add fresh water to the jar then drain off immediately to rinse.

4. Keep jar inverted at a slight angle so it continues to drain. Rinse sprouts 2-3 times a day until the desired size is reached.

Use them raw in salads or add them to stir frys and casseroles. This is a highly nutritious food that should be a staple in your diet.

cooking terms explained

chopping   Cut vegetables or fruit into approximately half-inch pieces.

dicing or mincing   Proceed as above for chopping then cut finer by rocking knife back and forth over cut pieces.

julienne cut   Cut vegetables into strips about 2 to 3 inches long by about 1/8 inch wide. This style of cutting vegetables is most commonly used for stir frying because it shortens cooking time.

puree   Process food in a blender or food processor until very smooth.

fold   Gently combining two mixtures, using a rubber spatula and a lifting motion. Avoid over-mixing.

whisk   Blending an ingredient into a mixture with the use of a wire whisk. This method helps the added ingredient to be incorporated into the mixture more thoroughly.

steaming   Put one inch water in a pot and set in a steamer basket. Arrange food evenly in basket (water should be beneath the food and not touching it). Cover the pot with a tight fitting lid and bring water to a boil. Lower heat just enough to keep water boiling. Steam food until desired tenderness is reached.

stir frying   With this method, foods are cooked quickly over moderately high heat in a small amount of oil while stirring constantly. A wok or large frying pan is suitable for this kind of cooking which helps to retain nutrients and brings out the flavors of the food.

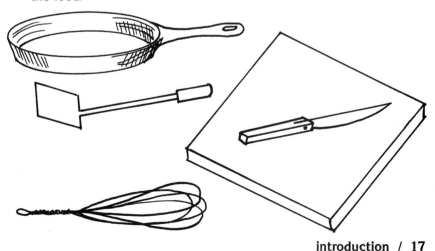

before you begin

1. Read each recipe through once or twice to familiarize yourself with each step before you begin.

2. Have all ingredients prepped and ready to go before starting the first step.

3. The preparation times given at the top of each recipe are average times for the average cook. They're meant to give an idea of how long each recipe will take from beginning to end. In recipes using cooked grains and beans, however, the prepping time given doesn't include their cooking time so allow for that difference.

4. For baked goods, have the baking pans lightly buttered and floured before mixing the ingredients.

5. If it's possible, don't cut the vegetables for a recipe until ready to cook. Exposure to the air means loss of vitamins, so if cut ahead enclose in a plastic bag.

6. Root vegetables like potatoes and carrots don't need to be peeled because they contain fewer chemicals than those grown above ground. Mineral and other vital elements lie close beneath the skin. Do scrub well, though, with a vegetable brush.

7. Steam rather than boil vegetables to retain as many nutrients as possible.

8. In recipes that call for grated lemon or orange rind, use organically grown fruit (free of pesticides) or scrub the fruit well before grating the rind.

9. Recipes that fit within the macrobiotic guide lines are denoted with a ☯ beside the recipe.

10. Spaces marked **"notes"** have been provided to alter recipes, make notes on new ideas, or document your dietary changes.

notes _____

_____

_____

breakfast

blueberry wheat cakes 21
buttermilk wheat cakes 21
granola deluxe. 20
maple nut millet 20
rice cereal with stewed plums ☯ 22

breads

basic bread. 28
cornbread 26
cranberry orange nut bread. 25
herbed tofu cornbread 27
pumpkin biscuits. 23
tea muffins 24
whole wheat chapatis. 28
whole wheat drop biscuits 24
zucchini bread 26

sandwiches

bean tostada 31
cream cheese pitas 29
croissant with brie. 30
falafel in pita 30
main meal sandwich 32
unclassical reuben 31

breakfast

maple nut millet

Yield: 4 servings
Prep: 15 min.
Cook: 20-30 min.

1. Bring to a boil in a saucepan and cook for 1 minute:

1½ cups apple juice   1 cup water
1 cup millet, rinsed

2. Add:

¼ cup raisins
¼ cup dried apricots,
    chopped

Cover and simmer for 20 minutes.

3. Mix in:

2 Tbsp. maple syrup   ½ tsp. nutmeg
½ tsp. cinnamon

You can serve this with chopped walnuts and a little milk or soymilk.

variation: If you omit the maple syrup and nutmeg, this can be considered a macrobiotic recipe.

Per serving: Calories: 202, Protein: 3 gm., Carbohydrates: 47 gm., Fat: 1 gm.

granola deluxe

Yield: 8 cups
Prep: 15 min.
Bake: 45 min.

Preheat oven to 375°.

1. Mix in a large bowl:

½ cup rolled oats   ½ cup oat bran
½ cup bran   ½ cup dried apples,
½ cup wheat germ   finely chopped
½ cup shredded coconut   12 oz. apple juice
           concentrate

Spread on a cookie sheet and bake on the middle rack of the oven for 30-35 minutes, stirring occasionally. Watch so it doesn't brown.

2. Mix together:

½ cup **walnuts, chopped**	½ cup **sunflower seeds**
½ cup **cashews, chopped**	½ cup **sesame seeds**
½ cup **pecans, chopped**	½ cup **almonds, chopped**

Spread on a cookie sheet and toast along with the grains and fruit for 10 to 15 minutes, stirring occasionally.

3. Mix everything together while still warm along with:
½ cup **raisins**
½ cup **dates, chopped**

Cool. Store in a tightly covered jar.

Per 1 cup serving: Calories: 513, Protein: 15 gm., Carbohydrates: 54 gm., Fat: 12 gm.

buttermilk wheat cakes

Yield: 8 pancakes
Prep: 10 min.

1. Mix in a medium mixing bowl until well combined:

½ cup **buttermilk**	1 Tbsp. **safflower oil**
1 **egg**	1 tsp. **vanilla**
2 Tbsp. **apple juice concentrate**	

2. Stir in:
6 rounded Tbsp. **whole wheat flour**
1 ½ tsp. **baking soda**

Spoon about ¼ cup of batter onto a seasoned skillet and cook for only 1 minute on each side. The batter should be thin; add more liquid if too thick. These are thin crepe-like cakes that are delicious with fresh fruit.

blueberry wheat cakes: Increase flour to ½ cup. Stir in 1 cup blueberries. Omit vanilla. These are thicker pancakes.

Per pancake: Calories: 50, Protein: 2 gm., Carbohydrates: 5 gm., Fat: 2 gm.

rice cereal with stewed plums

Yield: 3 servings
Prep: 15 min.
Cook: 30 min.

1. Combine in a saucepan and bring to a boil:

    1 lb. ripe plums, pitted   **½ cup cherry or apple**
    ½ cup water   **cider concentrate**

Reduce heat to low and simmer uncovered until fruit is cooked down and slightly thickened, about 30 minutes.

2. In another saucepan measure:

    3 cups cold water
    ½ tsp. sea salt (opt.)

Sprinkle in:

    1 cup rice cream cereal

Stir the cereal constantly over medium-high heat. Reduce heat and simmer for 20 minutes. Serve the plum sauce over the rice cereal. You can also top with yogurt and/or nuts.

Per serving: Calories: 274, Protein: 4 gm., Carbohydrates: 64 gm., Fat: 1 gm.

notes

breads

pumpkin biscuits

Yield: 40 biscuits
Prep: 4 ½ hours
Bake: 25 min.

1. Generously grease a large mixing bowl and lightly grease a baking sheet.

2. Combine in another large bowl and let stand until foamy and proofed, about 15 minutes:

½ cup warm water	½ tsp. honey
1½ envelopes dry yeast	

3. Stir in:

6¾ cups whole wheat flour	½ cup barley malt
1 cup pumpkin, cooked and mashed	2 tsp. ground ginger
¾ cup milk (or soy milk), scalded and cooled	1 tsp. sea salt
	½ tsp. nutmeg
	¼ tsp. cinnamon
	¼ tsp. allspice
	¼ tsp. cloves

4. Mix until soft dough forms. Transfer to floured work surface and knead until dough is smooth and elastic (adding more flour as necessary).

5. Place dough in a greased bowl, turning to coat entire surface. Cover and let rise in warm, draft free area until doubled in bulk, about 2½ hours.

6. Turn dough out onto floured work surface and roll to thickness of about 1 inch. Dip 2″ biscuit cutter into flour and cut out biscuits. Arrange close together on prepared baking sheet.

7. Cover and let rise until doubled in bulk, about 60 minutes. Preheat oven to 350°.

8. Bake until biscuits sound hollow when tapped on bottoms, about 25 minutes.

Per biscuit: Calories: 90, Protein: 3 gm., Carbohydrates: 18 gm., Fat: 0 gm.

whole wheat drop biscuits

See photo, opposite page 32.

Yield: 12 large biscuits
Prep: 5 min.
Bake: 20 min.

Preheat oven to 425°.

1. Combine in a medium bowl:
    2 cups whole wheat   **1 tsp. sea salt**
    pastry flour
    1 Tbsp. baking powder

2. Cut in until flour resembles a coarse meal:
    ½ cup butter or margarine

    You can also use several on/off pulses with a food processor to cut in the butter.

3. Add and mix thoroughly:
    ¾ cup low-fat milk or soy milk

4. Drop by a large spoonful onto a greased cookie sheet and bake for 18-20 minutes or until lightly browned.

Per biscuit: Calories: 142, Protein: 3 gm., Carbohydrates: 15 gm., Fat: 5 gm.

tea muffins

Yield: 12 muffins
Prep: 15 min.
Bake: 35-40 min.

Preheat oven to 350°. Grease 12 muffin tins.

1. Beat thoroughly in a medium bowl.
    2 ripe bananas, sliced   **1 egg**
    2 cups low-fat milk or   **1 tsp. vanilla**
    soy milk

    Set aside.

2. Sift together in a large bowl:
    2 cups brown rice flour   **1 tsp. cinnamon**
    1 cup rye flour   **1 tsp. nutmeg**
    1 tsp. baking soda   **1 tsp. clove**
    1 tsp. baking powder

Pour the wet mixture into the dry ingredients. Mix until just combined. Spoon into greased muffin tins, filling to the top. Bake 35-40 minutes.

Per muffin: Calories: 150, Protein: 4 gm., Carbohydrates: 30 gm., Fat: 1 gm.

cranberry orange nut bread

See photo, opposite page 32.

Yield: 16 slices
Prep: 10 min.
Bake: 35 min.

1. Place in a food processor or blender and process until coarsely chopped:
 1½ cups raw cranberries

Preheat oven to 350°.

2. Beat together:

2 eggs	1 tsp. vanilla
½ cup honey	grated rind of 1 orange
¾ cup orange juice	

Add cranberries and and mix well.

3. In a separate bowl combine:

1 cup whole wheat flour	1 tsp. baking soda
1 cup unbleached flour	½ tsp. sea salt
1 tsp. baking powder	

Stir in wet ingredients a little at a time until all is combined.

4. Stir in:
 ½ cup walnuts, chopped

5. Pour into a greased loaf pan and bake for 35 minutes or until a toothpick inserted in the center comes out clean.

Per slice: Calories: 127, Protein: 3 gm., Carbohydrates: 22 gm., Fat: 3 gm.

zucchini bread

Yield: 32 slices
Prep: 30 min.
Bake: 50-60 min.

Preheat oven to 350°.

1. In a large bowl, combine and whisk together thoroughly:

2½ cups soymilk (or lowfat milk)	¼ cup safflower oil
	1 Tbsp. vanilla
¾ cup honey	1 Tbsp. plus 1 tsp. egg
½ cup molasses	replacer (or 2 eggs)

Set aside.

2. In another large bowl, sift together:

1¾ cups rice flour	1 tsp nutmeg
1¾ cups rye flour	1 tsp. cinnamon
1½ tsp. baking soda	½ tsp. ground clove
1 tsp. baking powder	

Add to liquid mix a little at a time until just mixed.

3. Fold in:

2½ cups grated zucchini
¾ cups raisins

Divide batter into 2 greased loaf pans and bake for 50-60 minutes until a toothpick inserted in the center comes out clean.

Per slice: Calories: 117, Protein: 2 gm., Carbohydrates: 22 gm., Fat: 2 gm.

cornbread

Yield: 16 2″ x 3″ pieces
Prep: 20 min.
Bake: 18 min.

Preheat oven to 400°.

1. Sift into a large bowl:

1½ cups yellow cornmeal	1 Tbsp. baking powder
½ cup whole wheat flour	1 tsp. sea salt

2. In a separate bowl whisk together:

3 eggs	1 Tbsp. honey
1¼ cup milk	

3. Add liquid mix to the dry ingredients and stir until just combined.

Gently stir in:
    ¼ cup melted butter or margarine

Pour the batter into a greased 8″ X 12″ baking dish and bake for 15-20 minutes.

Per piece: Calories: 99, Protein: 3 gm., Carbohydrates: 12 gm., Fat: 3 gm.

herbed tofu cornbread

Yield: 8 large pieces
Prep: 10 min.
Bake: 50 min.

Preheat oven to 375°.

1. Blend in a food processor or blender:

1 lb. tofu	**½ cup corn oil**
1 cup soy milk	

2. Combine in a large bowl:

2 cups yellow cornmeal	**½ tsp. tarragon**
1 tsp. baking powder	**½ tsp. basil**
1 tsp. sea salt	**½ tsp. cayenne**

3. Stir the liquid mixture into the dry ingredients. Add to the batter:

1 medium carrot, minced	**1 cup corn**
1 small onion, finely chopped	

Spoon into a greased 8″ X 12″ baking dish and bake for 40-50 minutes or until a toothpick inserted into the center comes out clean.

Per serving: Calories: 416, Protein: 13 gm., Carbohydrates: 41 gm., Fat: 24 gm.

basic bread

Yield: 16 slices
Prep: 60 min.
Bake: 20-25 min.

Here is a very basic dough that can be used for any number of things like rolls, sweet buns or bread. Add raisins or seeds, even cinnamon, for a special taste.

1. Dissolve in 1¼ cups warm water:
　　　　1 Tbsp. dry yeast

2. Add:

1 Tbsp. sesame oil　　　　⅓ tsp. salt
1 Tbsp. honey or barley
malt

Mix well.

3. Sift in:

3 cups whole wheat flour
½ tsp. baking powder

Flour your counter, turn out dough and knead well, forming a soft, firm ball. Shape the dough, oil the top, place in oiled bread pan or baking sheet and place in a warm oven (pilot light) for 10 minutes. Cover with a damp cloth. After 10 minutes turn oven up to 400° and bake for 20-25 minutes. Tap lightly with a finger to test. If it gives a hollow sound, it's done.

Per serving: Calories: 87, Protein: 3 gm., Carbohydrates: 17 gm., Fat: 1 gm.

whole wheat chapatis

Yield: 10-12 chapatis
Prep: 60 min.

1. Dissolve in a large bowl:
　　　　1 cup water
　　　　½ tsp. sea salt

2. Add to make a kneadable dough:
　　　　2½ cups whole wheat
　　　　bread flour

3. Knead the dough on a floured surface, kneading in enough flour to make a smooth non-sticky dough. Cover with an inverted bowl and let rest 30 minutes. (This makes it easier to roll out.)

4. Cut the dough into 10-12 pieces of equal size. Roll out each piece of dough onto a floured surface until it's very thin. Cook chapatis on an unoiled, preheated skillet for about one minute on each side. Pat down with a paper towel while cooking.

Per chapati: Calories: 100, Protein: 4 gm., Carbohydrates: 21 gm., Fat: 0 gm.

sandwiches

cream cheese pitas

Yield: 8 open-face
sandwiches
Prep: 20 min.

See photo, opposite pg. 49.

1. Mix:

8 oz. softened cream cheese
¼ cup chopped parsley
2 Tbsp. chives or minced green onions

2 Tbsp. black olives, chopped
1 tsp. dill weed

Add a little milk if needed so it spreads easily.

2. Cut 4 pita breads in half, crosswise. Spread each with the cream cheese mix.

3. Sprinkle sandwiches with:
8 oz. alfalfa sprouts

Per serving: Calories: 387, Protein: 9 gm., Carbohydrates: 12 gm., Fat: 13 gm.

croissant with brie

Yield: 1 serving
Prep: 5 min.
Bake: 15 min.

Preheat oven to 300°.

1. Split:
> 1 whole wheat croissant

2. Spread on half:
> 1 Tbsp. softened brie

3. Top with:
> sliced cucumber
> 1 tsp. toasted slivered
> almonds

Put top on croissant, wrap in foil and heat for 15 minutes.

4. Open and fill with:
> ¼ cup watercress

Per serving: Calories: 229, Protein: 9 gm., Carbohydrates: 12 gm., Fat: 12 gm.

falafel in pita

Yield: 4 servings
Prep: 30 min.

1. Prepare according to package directions:
> 1-10 oz. box falafel mix

Shape into small balls or patties and brown in:
> 2 Tbsp. vegetable oil

2. For sauce, blend in a blender until smooth:
> ½ cup yogurt   1 clove garlic
> ¼ cup tahini   juice of 1 lemon

3. Stuff falafels into:
> 4 pita breads, cut in half
> to make pockets

4. Top each with:
> a tomato slice   the sauce
> 2 Tbsp. sprouts

Per serving: Calories: 598, Protein: 28 gm., Carbohydrates: 67 gm., Fat: 31 gm.

unclassical reuben

Yield: 2 servings
Grill: 3-5 min.

1. Butter both sides of:
>   **2 slices dark
>   pumpernickel bread**

2. Top slices with:
>   **2 oz. Swiss cheese**   **¼ cup Thousand Island
>   ½ cup sauerkraut**   **dressing**

3. Place under broiler and grill until cheese melts.

Per serving: Calories: 292, Protein: 11 gm., Carbohydrates: 21 gm., Fat: 14 gm.

bean tostada

Serves: 4
Prep: 20 min.

1. Blend in a food processor until smooth:
>   **2 cups cooked pinto   1 tsp. tamari
>   beans   ½ tsp. cayenne
>   2 Tbsp. cooking liquid   ½ tsp. garlic powder
>   2 tsp. cumin   ½ tsp. ginger**

2. Spread the bean dip on 4 crisp corn tostadas.

3. Cut into ¼" slices:
>   **1 avocado**

Line up the slices in one row across the bean dip.

4. Sprinkle the tostadas with:
>   **1 small onion, diced   ¾ cup cheddar, shredded
>   1 cup tomato, chopped   1 cup lettuce, shredded**

Serve with salsa.

Per serving: Calories: 257, Protein: 14 gm., Carbohydrates: 27 gm., Fat: 6 gm.

main meal sandwich

Yield: 8 servings
Prep: 30 min.

See photo, opposite page 81.

1. Cut in half lengthwise:
   1 large loaf sourdough or Italian bread

2. Heat in a large skillet:
   2 Tbsp. butter or margarine

Saute over medium high heat until lightly browned:
   8 oz. mushrooms, sliced

Remove mushrooms and add to the pan:
   1 Tbsp. butter or margarine
   2 medium onions, sliced

Cook until onions are wilted.

3. For spread, mix together:
   3 Tbsp. mayonnaise   **1 Tbsp. Dijon mustard**
   2 Tbsp. light or red miso

4. Cover bottom half of bread with spread. Top with:
   leaf lettuce   **1 red onion, sliced**
   2 tomatoes, sliced   **8 oz. mozzarella, sliced**
   1½ cups marinated red   **the sauteed onions**
      peppers, pg. 71   **the sauteed mushrooms**

Top with other half of loaf and cut into 8 slices.

Per serving: Calories: 578, Protein: 9 gm., Carbohydrates: 46 gm. Fat: 37 gm.

whole wheat drop biscuits, pg. 24, cranberry orange nut bread, pg.25

appetizers

baba ganouj 37
garlic-dill cheese dip 34
herbed yogurt cheese. 35
hummus ◐ 34
tempeh almond pate ◐. 36
tofu dip or sauce ◐ 35
tofu nut puree. 37
vegetable pate. 36
vegetarian sushi ◐. 38

Clockwise from top right: herbed yogurt cheese, pg. 35, garlic-dill cheese dip, pg. 34, hummus, pg. 34

hummus

Yield: 2½ cups
Prep: 15 min.

See photo, opposite page 33.

1. Combine in a blender or processor until smooth:

3 cloves garlic	⅓ cup tahini
2 cups cooked chick peas	¼ cup lemon juice
	¼ cup olive oil
½ cup cooking liquid *	1 tsp. sea salt

*add more if necessary

2. Serve on lettuce leaf as first course with pita bread or use as a spread on crackers or corn chips.

Per ½ cup serving: Calories: 356, Protein: 12 gm., Carbohydrates: 27 gm., Fat: 31 gm.

garlic-dill cheese dip

Yield: 1½ cups
Prep: 10 min.

See photo, opposite page 33.

1. Puree in a food processor until smooth:

1 small onion, chopped	3 cloves garlic, minced
8 oz. low fat cottage cheese	¼ cup fresh dill or 2 tsp. dried

2. Continue running processor and add a little at a time until smooth:

1½ cups soft, mild cheese, cubed
(Havarti, Meunster, Jack)

Chill well before serving.

Per 2 Tbsp. serving: Calories: 73, Protein: 6 gm., Carbohydrates: 1 gm., Fat: 3 gm.

notes

herbed yogurt cheese

Yield: 3 cups
Prep: 8 hours

See photo, opposite page 33.

1. Line a large sieve or strainer with 3 layers of rinsed cheese-cloth. Have cheesecloth hang over edges so it can be tied later.

Pour in:
3 quarts plain yogurt

Let this drain over a bowl or sink for 1-2 hours.

2. Tie the corners of the cloth together and continue to drain at room temperature for at least 8 hours, or overnight, until "cheese" is firm.

3. Combine in a bowl or decorative mold:

yogurt cheese	**2 Tbsp. fresh chives,**
2 Tbsp. fresh parsley,	**minced**
minced	**¼ cup green onion,**
2 Tbsp. fresh dill, minced	**minced**
or 2 tsp. dried	**2 Tbsp. fresh basil,**
	minced or 2 tsp. dried

Cover and refrigerate until well chilled. Use as a spread or dip.

Per ¼ cup serving: Calories: 139, Protein: 8 gm., Carbohydrates: 11 gm., Fat: 5 gm.

tofu dip or sauce

Yield: 2 cups
Prep: 15 min.

1. Combine in a blender and puree until smooth:

1 lb. tofu	**½ cup vegetable broth**
2 stalks celery, chopped	**½ cup toasted sesame**
1 clove garlic, minced	**seeds**
½ medium onion,	**¼ cup tamari**
chopped	**1 Tbsp. fresh grated**
	ginger

2. Chill. Serve with raw vegetables or crackers.

Per 2 Tbsp. serving: Calories: 54, Protein: 3 gm., Carbohydrates: 3 gm., Fat: 2 gm.

vegetable pate

Yield: 2 cups
Prep: 30 min.

1. Steam until very tender:
  1 cup green beans
  ½ cup carrot, chopped

2. Sauté together until limp:
  1 tsp. safflower oil
  1 medium onion, chopped

3. Combine above vegetables in processor and add:
  ¼ cup white wine   **¼ tsp. black pepper**
  2 Tbsp. mayonnaise   **¼ tsp. nutmeg**
  ¼ tsp. sea salt

Blend until smooth. Adjust seasonings to taste. Chill.

Per ¼ cup serving: Calories: 53, Protein: 1 gm., Carbohydrates: 4 gm., Fat: 3 gm.

tempeh almond pate

Yield: 3 cups
Prep: 30 min.

1. Steam for 10 minutes:
  2-8 oz. packages tempeh

Let cool slightly and cut into 1″ cubes. Set aside.

2. Simmer for 5 minutes:
  1 medium onion
  ½ cup dry white wine

3. Add to the above mixture:
  1½ cups mushrooms, sliced
  1 tsp. tamari

Cook over medium heat for 15 minutes.

4. Place in a food processor and grind until fine:
  1 cup almonds, roasted

5. Add tempeh and vegetables to the processor and puree along with the almonds until smooth. Chill well.

Per ¼ cup serving: Calories: 144, Protein: 10 gm., Carbohydrates: 11 gm., Fat: 3 gm.

tofu nut puree

Yield: 1½ cups
Prep: 5 min.

1. Place in a food processor and puree until smooth:

6 Tbsp. peanut butter	**2 Tbsp. barley miso**
2 Tbsp. honey	**½ lb. soft tofu**
2 Tbsp. lemon juice	

This is great as a cracker spread or melted over freshly steamed broccoli!

Per 2 Tbsp. serving: Calories: 75, Protein: 4 gm., Carbohydrates: 6 gm., Fat: 3 gm.

baba ganouj

Yield: 1½ cups
Prep: 15 min.
Cook: 45 min.

This is a delicious Middle Eastern dip.

Preheat oven to 350°.

1. Place on a cookie sheet and bake for 45 minutes:
3 medium eggplant

Allow to cool until easy to handle. Cut in half lengthwise, scrape eggplant out of skins. Chop eggplant and place in a food processor.

2. Add and puree until smooth:

⅓ cup tahini	**3 cloves garlic, minced**
¼ cup parsley, chopped	**½ tsp. sea salt**
¼ cup lemon juice	**¼ tsp. cayenne pepper**
¼ cup olive oil	

3. Chill. Serve with pita bread triangles or any mild chip or cracker.

Per serving: Calories: 127, Protein: 4 gm., Carbohydrates: 10 gm., Fat: 13 gm.

vegetarian sushi

Yield: 20 appetizers
Prep: 1 hour

1. Bring to a boil in a 1 quart covered pot:
>   **¹/₂ cup short grain brown**
>   **rice**
>   **1 ¹/₄ cups water**

Reduce heat and simmer until water is absorbed. Short grain rice is stickier than long grain and holds together better for sushi.

2. While rice is cooking, cut into julienne strips and set aside:
>   **1 small carrot**
>   **1 stalk celery**

Toast over a gas flame or bake in a 375° oven until bright green:
>   **4 sheets nori**

3. Lay one sheet of nori on a sushi mat* Spread ¹/₄ cup cooked rice over nori, leaving ¹/₂″ margins on all sides.

Sprinkle rice with:
>   **gomazio**
>   **rice vinegar or ume plum**
>   **vinegar**

At the end nearest you, lay pieces of one of the julienned vegetables end-to-end. Roll the nori over, tucking the end under the vegetable strip, then cover with the bamboo roller and roll forward, using pressure to determine how tightly the nori roll should wrap. Right before the end, remove extra rice and dampen the nori lightly with water. Roll closed. Keeping a sharp knife wet, slice through the roll at 1″ intervals. Arrange on a plate.

4. Squeeze together:
>   **¹/₂ tsp. firmly grated ginger**
>   **¹/₄ cup tamari**

Serve in a small bowl as a dip for the nori rolls.

* Sushi mats are available in many oriental or gourmet food stores.

Per appetizer: Calories: 15, Protein: 1 gm., Carbohydrates: 5 gm., Fat: 0 gm.

salads

california salad 47
daikon slaw ☯ 40
italian pasta salad 48
miso dressing ☯ 42
mixed grain salad with yogurt dressing 43
mock chicken almondine 44
mock chicken salad 44
mock tuna 45
rainbow pasta salad 48
sprout salad with miso dressing 40
sunflower potato salad 41
tempeh salad 42
tofu mayonnaise 40
waldorf salad 46

tofu mayonnaise

Yield: 1 cup
Prep: 5 min.

1. Puree in a food processor or blender until smooth:

1 lb. tofu	½ tsp. honey
2 Tbsp. lemon juice	½ tsp. Dijon mustard
2 Tbsp. olive oil	1 clove garlic, minced
1 tsp. white miso	

Per 2 Tbsp. serving: Calories: 78, Protein: 4 gm., Carbohydrates: 2 gm., Fat: 6 gm.

sprout salad with miso dressing

Yield: 4 servings
Prep: 10 min

1. Mix together:

½ cup lentil sprouts	½ cup adzuki bean sprouts
½ cup cowpea sprouts	½ cup alfalfa sprouts

Equal portions of any sprouts of your choice will do. Place on individual serving plates.

2. For the miso dressing, place in a blender and mix well:

¼ cup white miso	2 Tbsp. water
2 Tbsp. barley malt or rice syrup	2 tsp. rice vinegar
	1 tsp. tamari

Pour over sprouts and serve immediately.

Per serving: Calories: 125, Protein: 6 gm., Carbohydrates: 16 gm., Fat: 1 gm.

daikon slaw

Yield: 4 servings
Prep: 25 min.

1. Grate into a medium bowl:

2 medium carrots
½ medium daikon

Toss with:

½ cup parsley, chopped

2. Combine in a blender or whisk together:

¼ cup rice vinegar	1 Tbsp. tamari
¼ cup toasted sesame seeds	1 Tbsp. mirin
1 Tbsp. sesame oil	1 tsp. fresh ginger, grated (use juice by squeezing pulp)
1 Tbsp. toasted sesame oil	

Pour over vegetables and toss. Chill 30 minutes before serving.

Per serving: Calories: 138, Protein: 2 gm., Carbohydrates: 7 gm., Fat: 8 gm.

sunflower potato salad

Yield: 4 servings
Prep: 35 min

1. Scrub well, place in a large pot, cover with water and simmer until tender:

2½ lbs. Russet potatoes

Run cold water over them, drain. Set aside to cool.

2. Dice and set aside:

1 medium red onion
3 stalks celery

3. For dressing, combine in a small bowl:

½ cup mayonnaise	1 tsp. sea salt
2 tsp. fresh or dried dill weed	½ tsp. black pepper

4. Cut potatoes into chunks, combine with onions, celery and dressing, mixing well. Chill.

5. Right before serving top with:

½ cup toasted sunflower seeds.

Per serving: Calories: 497, Protein: 10 gm., Carbohydrates: 49 gm., Fat: 19 gm.

tempeh salad

Yield: 4 servings
Prep: 25 min.

1. Steam in a steamer basket for 15 minutes:
8 oz. soy tempeh

Cool. Cut into ½″ cubes. Set aside.

2. Place in a small bowl:
½ cup arame

Rinse three times with fresh water.

3. Combine in a bowl:

2 scallions, chopped	¼ cup parsley, chopped
1 stalk celery, chopped	the tempeh cubes
½ medium carrot, shredded	arame
½ cup adzuki sprouts	

4. Toss with Miso Dressing (see below). Chill before serving.

Per serving: Calories: 108, Protein: 12 gm., Carbohydrates: 12 gm., Fat: 1 gm.

miso dressing ☯

Yield: ¾ cup
Prep: 5 min.

1. Place in a blender and blend until smooth:

1 clove garlic, minced - optional	¼ cup apple juice
½ small onion, minced	3 Tbsp. rice vinegar
⅓ cup white miso	

Per 2 Tbsp. serving: Calories: 42, Protein: 1 gm., Carbohydrates: 9 gm., Fat: 0 gm.

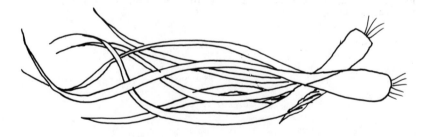

mixed grain salad with yogurt dressing

Yield: 6 servings (side dish) or 3 servings (main meal)

Prep: 1 hour

1. Simmer over low heat until tender and water is absorbed:

3½ cups water	½ cup triticale
½ cup wheatberries	½ cup buckwheat

In another pot, simmer over low heat until water is absorbed:

2½ cups water	½ cup barley
½ cup brown rice	

2. For dressing, blend in a blender until well combined:

1 cup plain yogurt	1 tsp. ginger
¼ cup red wine vinegar	1 tsp. garlic
2 Tbsp. prepared mustard	

3. Have ready:

1 cup mung bean sprouts	½ cup celery, chopped
½ cup scallions, chopped	½ red pepper, chopped
½ cup jicama or cooked beets, chopped	½ cup parsley, chopped

When grains are at room temperature, combine them with the vegetables and dressing in a large bowl. Chill.

Per side dish serving: Calories: 223, Protein: 9 gm., Carbohydrates: 44 gm., Fat: 2 gm.

notes

mock chicken salad

Yield: 4 servings
Prep: 20 min.

1. Steam for 10 minutes:
      8 oz. soy tempeh, thawed

Cool. Cut into ½″ cubes or grate on large holes of grater. Set aside in a medium mixing bowl.

2. Combine with the tempeh:
2 stalks celery, chopped
2 Tbsp. red or green
    onion, minced

2 Tbsp. parsley, minced
2 Tbsp. pickle relish
    (optional)

3. Mix in:
5 Tbsp. mayonnaise
1 tsp. prepared mustard

1 tsp. tamari
½ tsp. garlic powder

Chill. Serve on lettuce leaves.

mock chicken almondine: Add ½ cup slivered roasted almonds before serving.

Per serving: Calories: 281, Protein: 15 gm., Carbohydrates: 14 gm., Fat: 16 gm.

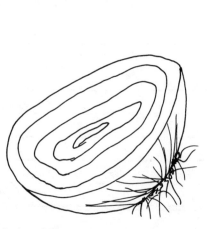
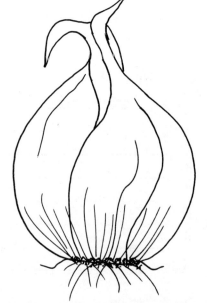

mock tuna

Yield: 4 servings
Prep: 20 min.

1. Puree in a food processor until a fine meal consistency is reached:

      1½ cups cooked
       chickpeas
      1½ cups cooked
       soybeans

Put in a medium mixing bowl.

2. Add to beans:

    2 stalks celery, chopped   1 clove garlic, minced
    ½ medium onion, diced

3. Stir in and mix well:

    ½ cup mayonnaise   2 tsp. tamari
    ¼ cup pickle relish   1½ tsp. kelp powder
    ¼ cup nutritional yeast   ⅛ tsp. black pepper

Chill.

Per serving: Calories: 475, Protein: 16 gm., Carbohydrates: 42 gm., Fat: 18 gm.

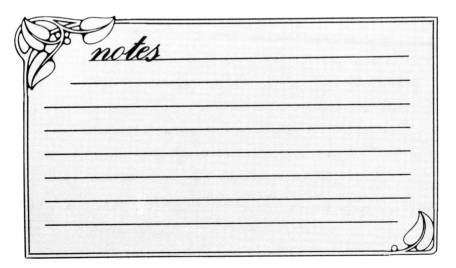

notes

waldorf salad

Yield: 8 servings
Prep: 25 min.

1. Toss together in a large bowl:

6 tart apples, chopped	**½ cup walnuts, chopped**
1 cup pineapple chunks	**½ cup celery, chopped**
(optional)	**½ cup carrots, grated**
½ cup raisins	

Set aside.

2. Whisk together in a medium bowl:

1 cup plain yogurt	**2 Tbsp. honey**
¼ cup orange juice	**juice of 1 lemon**

Toss with fruit. Chill.

Per serving: Calories: 27, Protein: 4 gm., Carbohydrates: 39 gm., Fat: 6 gm.

notes

california salad

Yield: 4 servings
Prep: 30 min.

See photo, opposite page 48.

1. Boil until tender (about 15 minutes):
4 small beets

To peel, run cold water over beets while squeezing off the skin. Cut each one into quarters and set aside. Drained canned beets can be used, cut in half.

2. For dressing, combine in a blender with several on/off pulses until well blended:

⅓ cup red wine vinegar　　**¼ tsp. black pepper**
⅓ cup olive oil　　　　　　**1 clove garlic, minced**
¼ cup fresh basil,
chopped fine or 1 tsp.
dried

3. Have ready:

1-4 oz. jar marinated　　**1 head Bibb lettuce**
artichoke hearts,　　　**1 ripe avocado**
drained　　　　　　　　**1 cup alfalfa sprouts**

Arrange on a platter or on individual serving plates bite-size pieces of lettuce, the beets, artichoke hearts and avocado slices around the edges with the sprouts in the center. Pass the dressing.

Per serving: Calories: 134, Protein: 16 gm., Carbohydrates: 13 gm., Fat: 4 gm.

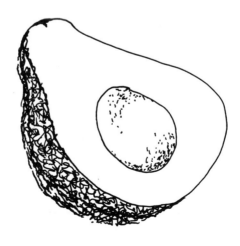

rainbow pasta salad

Yield: 8 servings
Prep: 35 min.

See photo on facing page.

1. Chop into ¼" pieces:

2 medium zucchini

1 medium red onion, minced

1 medium red pepper

1 medium green pepper

Set aside.

2. Bring to a boil:

2 quarts water

Then add:

3½ cups rainbow spiral pasta

Cook to al dente (still chewy-not too soft and mushy). Drain, run under cold water to cool, drain again and place in a large mixing bowl.

3. For dressing, combine in a blender until thoroughly mixed:

½ cup red wine vinegar

½ cup olive oil

1 tsp. basil

1 tsp. tarragon

1 tsp. oregano

1 tsp. sea salt

1 tsp. pepper

2 cloves garlic, minced

4. Combine the vegetables and pasta, tossing gently. Pour dressing over everything and toss well. Chill.

italian pasta salad: Before serving, add 1 cup of grated parmesan or romano cheese for a true Italian treat!

Per serving: Calories: 275, Protein: 6 gm., Carbohydrates: 33 gm., Fat: 14 gm.

Top: california salad, pg. 47, Bottom: rainbow pasta salad (this page)

soups

carrot-yogurt soup 56
cool avocado soup 50
curried split pea soup 51
fruit soup 51
humble miso soup ☯ 52
land & sea vegetable soup ☯ 53
miso wakame soup ☯ 52
mushroom-barley soup ☯ 55
pumpkin soup 54
spicy pea soup 51
spicy tomato-peanut soup 54
zucchini yogurt soup 50

carrot-yogurt soup, pg. 56, cream cheese pita, pg. 29

cool avocado soup

Yield: 4 servings
Prep: 15 min.

1. Grind in a food processor or blender to a fine meal:
   ½ cup cashews, roasted

2. Add to the processor and puree until smooth:

2 ripe avocados	1½ Tbsp. lemon juice
2½ cups water	1 tsp. onion powder
½ cup buttermilk	½ clove garlic, minced

Chill.

Per serving: Calories: 274, Protein: 6 gm., Carbohydrates: 15 gm., Fat: 6 gm.

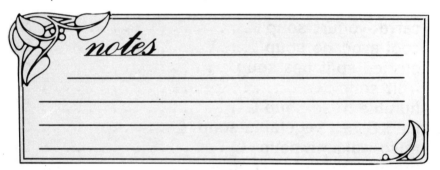

notes

zucchini yogurt soup

Yield: 3 cups
Prep: 10 min.
Cook: 15 min.

1. Sauté in a skillet until onions are tender:

1 medium onion, chopped	2 large zucchini, chopped
2 cloves garlic, minced	2 Tbsp. sesame oil
	½ tsp. white pepper

2. Place sautéed vegetables in a blender or food processor and add:
   1 pint low-fat plain
   yogurt (room temp.)

Blend until smooth. Serve immediately or warm gently over medium low heat.
Do not allow to boil.

Per serving: Calories: 267, Protein: 13 gm., Carbohydrates: 31 gm., Fat: 12 gm.

curried split pea soup

Yield: 4 servings
Cook: 1 hour

1. Combine in a medium soup pot and bring to a boil:

    3 cups water   **1 vegetable bouillon cube**
    2 cups yellow split peas   **1 medium onion,**
        chopped

2. Combine in a blender and blend for about 5 seconds:

    1½ cups hot water   **1 Tbsp. curry powder**
    1 cup grated coconut,
    unsweetened

Add this to the soup pot. Turn heat to medium-low, cover pan and simmer for 40 minutes or until peas are tender.

You can continue cooking uncovered to allow soup to thicken. Then mix with 2 fried onions and serve as a side dish called dahl. Excellent with sesame sticks.

spicy pea soup: For a spicier soup, add a clove of minced garlic and 3 crushed chili peppers.

Per serving: Calories: 341, Protein: 21 gm., Carbohydrates: 56 gm., Fat: 4 gm.

fruit soup

Yield: 6 servings
Prep: 15 min.

1. Blend in a blender or food processor until smooth:

    5 nectarines, chopped   **1 cup plain yogurt**
    2 bananas, sliced   **1 tsp. dried mint**
    1 cup apple juice   **½ tsp. cinnamon**
    1 cup buttermilk   **½ tsp. allspice**
    ½ cup almonds, toasted   **juice of 1 lemon**

You may want to blend in batches. Chill for 1-2 hours.

Per serving: Calories: 265, Protein: 8 gm., Carbohydrates: 40 gm., Fat: 4 gm.

humble miso soup

Yield: 1 cup
Cook: 1 min.

1. Dissolve:

1 tsp. white miso
1 cup hot water

Do not boil after miso is added. Garnish with chopped scallion if you wish. A traditional oriental breakfast.

Per 1 cup serving: Calories: 13, Protein: 1 gm., Carbohydrates: 3 gm., Fat: 0 gm.

miso wakame soup

Yield: 4 servings
Cook: 10 min.
Prep: 15 min.

1. Bring to a boil:

4 cups water
½ cup dried wakame

Simmer for 10 minutes. You can add for the last couple of minutes of cooking.:

½ cup carrots, julienned   **2 scallion stalks,**
½ cup mushrooms,   **chopped**
   sliced

2. Remove ½ cup broth and dissolve into it:

4 tsp. red miso

Add back to the soup and serve immediately. Top with chopped scallions.

Per serving: Calories: 26, Protein: 1 gm., Carbohydrates: 5 gm., Fat: 0 gm.

land & sea vegetable soup

Yield: 6 servings
Prep: 15 min.
Cook: 45 min.

1. Bring to a boil in a large soup pot:

6 cups water
5 shitake mushrooms,
   rinsed and sliced

½ cup adzuki beans,
   cooked
½ cup hijiki seaweed,
   rinsed
1 tsp. toasted sesame oil

Reduce heat to low and simmer for 15 minutes.

2. Add to soup:

4 scallions, chopped
1 cup snow peas, sliced
   in half
2 Tbsp. white miso,
   dissolved in 1 cup of
   the broth

1 Tbsp. tamari
1 tsp. ginger, grated

Turn off the heat, cover, and let sit for 10 minutes. Serve.

Per serving: Calories: 54, Protein: 3 gm., Carbohydrates: 9 gm., Fat: 1 gm.

notes

pumpkin soup

Yield: 3-4 servings
Prep: 20 min.
Cook: 30 min.

1. Place in a steamer basket:
> 1 medium pumpkin, cut
> in quarters

Cover and steam until tender. Cool.

2. Sauté until tender:
> 1 medium onion,
> chopped
> 2 Tbsp. sesame oil

3. Scoop pumpkin from shell and place in blender or processor with the sautéed onion. Slowly add and puree until smooth:

2 cups milk	½ tsp. nutmeg
2 Tbsp. tamari	½ tsp. black pepper
1 tsp. allspice	

Reheat over low heat and serve with a sprinkle of nutmeg.

Per serving: Calories: 324, Protein: 10 gm., Carbohydrates: 39 gm., Fat: 13 gm.

spicy tomato-peanut soup

Yield: 2-3 servings
Prep: 15 min.
Cook: 10 min.

1. Puree in a blender:
> 4 large tomatoes,
> chopped
> ½ medium onion,
> chopped

2. Add to above mixture:

½ cup roasted peanuts,	½ tsp. cayenne pepper
finely ground	
2 Tbsp. tamari	

3. Pour into a saucepan and heat gently. Garnish with a dollop of yogurt or sour cream.

Per serving: Calories: 292, Protein: 14 gm., Carbohydrates: 25 gm., Fat: 6 gm.

mushroom-barley soup

Yield: 4 servings
Prep: 10 min.
Cook: 30 min.

1. Sauté until tender:
    1 Tbsp. sesame oil
    1 medium onion,
      chopped

2. Add:
    ½ cup barley, rinsed
Sauté until the barley begins to brown, stirring frequently.
Then add:
    2 cups mushrooms,
      sliced
    2 Tbsp. tamari
Cook until mushrooms are tender.

3. Combine with above:
    4 cups hot water
Bring to a boil. Reduce heat to medium-low and cook until
barley is tender (about 30 minutes).

Per serving: Calories: 144, Protein: 4 gm., Carbohydrates: 25 gm., Fat: 4
gm.

notes

carrot-yogurt soup

Yield: 8 servings
Prep: 15 min.
Cook: 45 min.

See photo opposite page 49.

1. In a large soup pot sauté until soft:

1 medium onion, chopped	4 Tbsp. butter or margarine
1 clove garlic, minced	

2. Add:

½ tsp. mustard seed	½ tsp. sea salt
½ tsp. tumeric	¼ tsp. cayenne
½ tsp. ginger	¼ tsp. cinnamon
½ tsp. cumin	

Cook for several minutes over medium heat, stirring constantly.

3. Add to soup pot:

1 lb. carrots, sliced	2 cups water
1 Tbsp. lemon juice	

Cover tightly and simmer until carrots are tender (about 30 minutes).

4. Puree in a blender in several batches:

the cooked carrots
the cooking liquid

5. Return the puree to the pot and whisk in:

2 cups low-fat plain yogurt	1 Tbsp. honey
2 Tbsp. fresh dill or 1 tsp. dried	¼ tsp. black pepper

Heat gently but do not boil. Ladle into soup bowls and sprinkle with dill.

Per serving: Calories: 125, Protein: 4 gm., Carbohydrates: 13 gm., Fat: 5 gm.

sauces

cranberry sauce ☯ 61
dried fruit jam 64
fig sauce 62
fruit chutney 63
fruit sauce 62
green sauce 59
hearty tomato sauce 58
italian tomato sauce 58
lo-cal mock sour cream 59
mango chutney 63
miso-pesto sauce ☯ 60
miso-tahini sauce ☯ 60
mushroom sauce 58
onion-fruit relish 64
orange sesame sauce 60
summer tomato basil sauce 59
sweet potato sauce 61

italian tomato sauce

Yield: 3 cups
Prep: 15 min.
Cook: 30 min.

1. Sauté over medium high heat, stirring frequently, until onions are tender:

2 Tbsp. olive oil
2 medium onions,
 chopped

2 cloves garlic, minced

2. Add to above mixture and simmer for 30 minutes:

4 cups tomatoes,
 chopped
1 cup mushrooms, sliced
2 green peppers,
 chopped
2 Tbsp. tomato paste

1 Tbsp. tamari
1 Tbsp. honey or barley
 malt
2 tsp. oregano
1 tsp. basil
2 bay leaves

hearty tomato sauce: Add ½ cup TVP after tomato mix has simmered and allow to stand for 15 more minutes. Serve over 1 pound cooked pasta.

Per 1 cup serving: Calories: 222, Protein: 6 gm., Carbohydrates: 31 gm., Fat: 9 gm.

mushroom sauce

Yield: 2 cups
Prep: 10 min.
Cook: 15 min.

1. Combine in a saucepan and heat to boiling:

2 cups mushrooms,
 sliced
1 medium onion,
 chopped
½ cup dry white wine or
 vegetable broth

2 Tbsp. tamari
1 tsp. seasoning mix
1 clove garlic, minced

2. Remove ½ cup cooking liquid and whisk in:

1 Tbsp. arrowroot powder

Return liquid to the mushroom mixture and heat for 5 minutes more, stirring occasionally. Serve on brown rice or steamed vegetables.

Per ½ cup serving: Calories: 64, Protein: 2 gm., Carbohydrates: 9 gm., Fat: 0 gm.

summer tomato basil sauce

Yield: 1½ cups
Prep: 15 min.

1. Place in a blender and puree until smooth:

1 cup plain yogurt
2 Tbsp. chopped fresh
basil

2 Tbsp. olive oil
2 medium tomatoes, cut
up

Refrigerate. Serve as a dip for raw vegetables or over a pasta salad.

Per ½ cup serving: Calories: 151, Protein: 4 gm., Carbohydrates: 8 gm., Fat: 11 gm.

green sauce

Yield: 3/4 cup
Prep: 15 min.

1. Place in a blender and puree until smooth:

8 cherry tomatoes or 1
large tomato, cut up
4 scallions, chopped
1 clove garlic, mashed
⅓ cup lemon juice

¼ cup water
1 Tbsp. white miso
2 tsp. spirulina
½ tsp. cayenne pepper

2. Serve over grated veggies (carrot, zucchini, daikon), sprouts, chopped cauliflower and celery for a refreshing summer salad. Sprinkle with toasted sunflower seeds.

Per ¼ cup serving: Calories: 30, Protein: 1 gm., Carbohydrates: 7 gm., Fat: 0 gm.

lo·cal mock sour cream

Yield: 1 cup
Prep: 10 min.

1. Blend in a blender or food processor until smooth:

½ cup low-fat cottage
cheese
½ cup low-fat yogurt

Per 2 tbsp. serving: Calories: 19, Protein: 3 gm., Carbohydrates: 1 gm., Fat: 0 gm.

miso-pesto sauce

Yield: 1 cup
Prep: 15 min.

1. Place in a food processor and puree until the mixture becomes a smooth, thick paste:

3 cloves garlic, chopped
2 cups fresh basil leaves
1 cup walnuts, chopped

½ cup parsley, coarsely chopped
½ cup olive oil
¼ cup white miso

2. Toss with hot pasta of choice. Spiral noodles make a nice chilled pasta salad with the addition of chopped fresh veggies (broccoli, cauliflower, red pepper, onion, etc.) Toss with cooked spaghetti squash. Spread over French bread and run under the broiler.

Per ¼ cup serving: Calories: 482, Protein: 8 gm., Carbohydrates: 42 gm., Fat: 45 gm.

miso-tahini sauce

Yield: 1½ cups
Prep: 15 min.

1. Place in a blender and puree until smooth:

1 cup tahini
¼ cup white miso
2 Tbsp. tamari
1 Tbsp. rice vinegar

½ tsp. fresh grated ginger
1 clove garlic, minced
water*

*Use enough water to make it a smooth, thick sauce. Serve over brown rice.

Per ¼ cup serving: Calories: 321, Protein: 10 gm., Carbohydrates: 11 gm., Fat: 54 gm.

orange sesame sauce

Yield: 1 cup
Prep: 5 min.

1. Combine in a bowl and mix well:

1 cup mayonnaise
½ cup orange juice
2 Tbsp. toasted sesame seeds

1½ Tbsp. toasted sesame oil
1 Tbsp. Dijon mustard

Serve over steamed asparagus or broccoli. Allow sauce to come to room temperature if refrigerated.

Per 2 Tbsp. serving: Calories: 242, Protein: 1 gm., Carbohydrates: 3 gm., Fat: 20 gm.

cranberry sauce ☯

Yield: 2 cups
Prep: 5 min.
Cook: 25-30 min.

1. Bring to a boil in a medium saucepan:

1 cup water   grated rind of 1 orange
¾ cup honey or ½ cup
  barley malt plus ½ cup
  rice syrup

2. Add:

12 oz. whole cranberries,
  rinsed

Cook over medium-high heat until the berries pop open.
Reduce heat and simmer for 10 minutes.

3. Remove from heat and allow to cool. Puree half of the mixture
and then mix with the rest. Chill before serving.

Per 2 Tbsp. serving: Calories: 58, Protein: 0 gm., Carbohydrates: 16 gm.,
Fat: 0 gm.

sweet potato sauce

Yield: 1½ cups
Prep: 10 min.
Cook: 20 min.

1. Scrub and cut into 1″ slices:

1 large sweet potato (red
  garnets are best)

Steam in a steamer basket until tender (about 15 minutes).

2. Place in a food processor along with enough cooking liquid to
make good sauce consistency:

the cooked potato
2 Tbsp. lemon juice

Puree until smooth. Serve over steamed broccoli or cauliflower
with toasted sunflower seeds as a topping.

Per ¼ cup serving: Calories: 28, Protein: 1 gm., Carbohydrates: 7 gm.,
Fat: 0 gm.

fig sauce

Yield: 1½ cups
Prep: 5 min.
Cook: 45 min.

1. Place in a saucepan and heat to boiling:

2 cups red wine	1 Tbsp. orange peel,
1 cup vegetable broth	slivered
½ lb. dried figs, cut in	1 Tbsp. lemon peel,
quarters	slivered
⅓ cup honey or barley	1 tsp. cloves, powdered
malt	½ tsp. thyme
	2 cloves garlic, minced

Continue to boil for 5 minutes. Lower heat and simmer for 45 minutes, covered.

2. Puree half of the mixture and return it to the saucepan. Wonderful served over Tofu Nut Loaf (pg. 80) for the holidays.

Per ¼ cup serving: Calories: 228, Protein: 1 gm., Carbohydrates: 45 gm., Fat: 0 gm.

fruit sauce

Yield: 1 cup
Prep: 10 min.
Cook: 15 min.

1. Melt in a medium saucepan over medium high heat:

¼ cup butter or
margarine

2. Add to the melted butter and sauté for 5 minutes, stirring often:

½ cup assorted chopped	½ cup assorted chopped
dried fruits (dates, figs,	nuts (walnuts, pecans,
raisins, papaya,	cashews, hazelnuts)
apricots)	

3. Add, stirring frequently:

⅓ cup apple juice
concentrate or barley
malt.

Cook until mixture thickens (about 8 minutes). Serve with ice cream, cake, yogurt, cottage cheese, breakfast cereal.

Per 2 Tbsp. serving: Calories: 146, Protein: 2 gm., Carbohydrates: 13 gm., Fat: 8 gm.

fruit chutney

Yield: 3 cups
Prep: 15 min.
Cook: 1½ hours

1. Combine in a large saucepan, bring to a boil and cook for 5 minutes:

4 dried chili peppers, crushed	**½ cup raisins**
½ cup dried apricots, chopped	**½ cup apple cider vinegar**
½ cup dried apples, chopped	**1 tsp. cinnamon**
½ cup pitted prunes, chopped	**1 tsp. allspice**
	½ tsp. cloves

2. Add:

2 cups apple juice
2 cups water

3. Return to a boil. Reduce heat to low and simmer for 1½ hours, stirring occasionally. Cool before serving.

Per 2 Tbsp.serving: Calories: 25, Protein: 0 gm., Carbohydrates: 7 gm., Fat: 0 gm.

mango chutney

Yield: 2 cups
Prep: 15 min.
Cook: 1 hour

1. Place in a medium saucepan and bring to a boil:

3-4 ripe mangos, peeled and sliced off the pit	**½ cup apple cider vinegar**
3 cloves garlic, minced	**¼ cup raisins**
3 dried chili peppers, crushed	**2 Tbsp. honey**
	½ Tbsp. grated ginger

2. Reduce heat to low and simmer for at least 1 hour, stirring occasionally. Keep covered and refrigerated. Serve chilled with a curried main dish.

Per 2 Tbsp. serving: Calories: 44, Protein: 0 gm., Carbohydrates: 12 gm., Fat: 0 gm.

onion-fruit relish

Yield: 2 cups
Prep: 10 min.
Cook: 30 min.

1. In a saucepan bring to a boil:
> 1 quart water
> 1 lb. pearl onions,
> unpeeled

Boil for 1 minute. Drain onions, run under cold water and squeeze them at one end to pop them out of their skins.

2. In a medium saucepan combine and bring to a boil:

1 cup white wine	¼ cup tomato paste
⅓ cup currants	2 Tbsp. parsley
⅓ cup apricots, chopped	½ tsp. thyme
⅓ cup dried dates, chopped	2 bay leaves
½ cup wine vinegar	pepper

Lower heat and simmer uncovered until liquid is reduced by half.

3. Add:
> blanched onions

Toss until evenly coated. Heat through and serve.

Per 2 Tbsp. serving: Calories: 43, Protein: 1 gm., Carbohydrates: 8 gm., Fat: 0 gm.

dried fruit jam

Yield: 1 cup
Prep: 10 min.
Cook: 45 min.

1. Combine in a medium saucepan and bring to a boil:

1½ cups apple juice	½ tsp. cloves, powdered
½ cup Adriatic figs	¼ tsp. cinnamon
½ cup unsulphered apricots	¼ tsp. allspice

2. Reduce heat to low and simmer for 45 minutes. Allow to cool and then puree the mixture in a food processor until almost smooth.

Per 2 Tbsp. serving: Calories: 42, Protein: 0 gm., Carbohydrates: 10 gm., Fat: 0 gm.

side dishes

braised chestnuts & brussels sprouts ☯.... 66
cardamom carrots 66
creamed spinach 68
hot garlic eggplant 70
marinated red peppers 71
pasta shells in mushroom garlic sauce 71
potatoes boulangere 69
stuffed butternut squash 67
tsimmes 68

stuffings

almond rice pilaf ☯ 74
apple-date stuffing 75
cornbread stuffing 72
fruited cous-cous stuffing 73
wild rice stuffing 72

cardamom carrots

Yield: 6 servings
Prep: 15 min.
Cool: 15 min.

1. Steam until crisp-tender:
>   2 lbs. carrots, sliced ¼"
>   thick

2. Melt over medium heat:
>   ¼ cup unsalted butter or
>   margarine

Add carrots and:

>   1 Tbsp. honey or barley   4 cardamom pods, hulled
>   malt   and crushed or ½ tsp.
>   1½ Tbsp, orange peel,   powdered cardamom
>   grated

Cook for 2-3 minutes, coating evenly. Season with sea salt to taste.

Per serving: Calories: 135, Protein: 2 gm., Carbohydrates: 16 gm., Fat: 5 gm.

braised chestnuts & brussels sprouts ☯

Yield: 4 servings
Prep: 30 min
Cook: 40 min

1. Sauté in a large pan:
>   1 lb. chestnuts, peeled
>   2 Tbsp. sesame oil

Toss to coat.

2. Dissolve:
>   ⅓ cup white miso
>   1½ cups water

Add to chestnuts. Cover and simmer until tender (20-25 minutes).

3. Wash, trim and cut an X in the stem ends of:
>   1 lb. Brussels sprouts

Steam until tender (5-7 minutes), drain and rinse under cold water to stop the cooking process.

4. When chestnuts are tender, increase heat to medium-high, add Brussels sprouts and cook until liquid reduces to a glaze (10 minutes). Add to taste:
>   **sea salt and pepper**

variation: Use almonds or Brazil nuts instead of chestnuts.

Per serving: Calories: 317, Protein: 11 gm., Carbohydrates: 66 gm., Fat: 1 gm.

stuffed butternut squash

Yield: 4 servings
Prep: 15 min.
Bake: 1 hour

Preheat oven to 350°.

1. Cut in half lengthwise and scoop out the seeds:
>   **1 medium butternut**
>   **squash**

2. Stir together until smooth:
>   **½ cup tahini**   **1 Tbsp. honey or barley**
>   **¼ cup apple juice**   **malt**

Add until well combined:
>   **1 cup dried fruit and nut**
>   **mix**

Stuff the squash with this mixture, rounding the stuffing over the top.

3. Place squash in a casserole pan with:
>   **½ cup water in the**
>   **bottom**

Cover with aluminum foil and bake for 50 minutes. Remove cover and bake for another 10 minutes.

Per serving: Calories: 266, Protein: 8 gm., Carbohydrates: 30 gm., Fat: 24 gm.

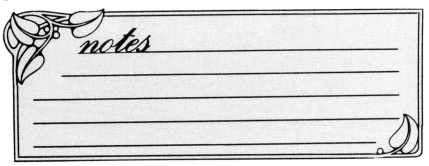

notes

creamed spinach

Yield: 2 servings
Prep: 15 min.
Cook: 15 min.

1. Sauté over medium-high heat until tender:
  2 tsp. sesame oil
  1 medium onion,
    chopped

2. Dissolve:
  ½ cup milk or soy milk   2 Tbsp. powdered milk or
  2 Tbsp. arrowroot   soy powder
  Add to the onions and stir well over medium heat.

3. Add to onions and cook until wilted:
  1 lb. spinach, washed

4. Add to spinach and onions:
  1 Tbsp. lemon juice   ½ tsp. white pepper
  ½ tsp. nutmeg
  Sauté for 5 minutes. Serve immediately.

Per serving: Calories: 220, Protein: 13 gm., Carbohydrates: 29 gm., Fat: 6 gm.

tsimmes

Yield: 4-6 servings
Prep: 50 min.
Bake: 30 min.

This is a delicious traditional Jewish holiday dish.

1. In a large skillet sauté until tender:
  1 Tbsp. sesame oil
  1 medium onion,
    chopped

2. Add and cook for 10 minutes, stirring frequently:
  2 carrots, chopped   2 tart apples, chopped
  3 large sweet potatoes,
    chopped

3. Add to skillet:
  15 pitted prunes   ½ tsp. cinnamon
  1½ cups orange juice   ½ tsp. nutmeg
  juice of 2 lemons   ½ tsp. ground cloves
  Stir to combine, cover and simmer until tender (about 30 minutes).

4. Preheat oven to 350°.
Turn the cooked mixture into a large bowl and combine with:
1 cup cheddar cheese,
shredded

5. Pour into a casserole pan and top with:
1 cup walnuts, chopped
Bake for 30 minutes.

Per serving: Calories: 501, Protein: 14 gm., Carbohydrates: 59 gm., Fat: 21 gm.

potatoes boulangere

Yield: 6 servings
Prep: 20 min.
Bake: 30 min.

1. Slice as thinly as possible (⅛″ to ¼″):
8 medium potatoes,
scrubbed
Keep the potatoes you've sliced in cold water to prevent browning while you finish the others.

2. Have ready:
1 ¼ cup gruyere or   **¼ tsp. black pepper**
Swiss cheese, grated   **6 Tbsp. butter**
1 tsp. sea salt

3. Preheat oven to 425°.
Drain potatoes. Butter a 9″ X 12″ X 2″ casserole pan and arrange half the potatoes in the pan.

4. Sprinkle with half the cheese, salt, pepper and dot with half the butter. Repeat with the remaining potatoes and other ingredients.

5. Mix together:
1 cup vegetable bouillon
1 Tbsp. white miso
Pour over the pan of potatoes and bake until tender (about 30 minutes).

Per serving: Calories: 299, Protein: 10 gm., Carbohydrates: 25 gm., Fat: 12 gm.

hot garlic eggplant

Yield: 4 servings
Prep: 20 min.
Cook: 30 min.

This is a nice side dish for an Indian feast or can be a meal in itself when served over spinach noodles with roasted pine nuts, chopped tomatoes and crumbled feta cheese.

1. Dice into ½″ cubes:
   1½ lbs. eggplant, peeled
   Place in a large bowl and generously sprinkle with salt. Set aside for about 30 minutes.

2. Sauté over medium-high heat for 2 minutes, stirring constantly:

3 Tbsp. peanut oil	**1 red pepper, roasted**
10 cloves garlic, minced	**(opt.)**
1 Tbsp. chili peppers, crushed	**½ tsp. grated ginger root**

Lower heat and add, cooking until tender:
   1 medium onion, chopped

3. Whisk together in a small bowl:

½ cup dry red wine	**2 tsp. toasted sesame oil**
3 Tbsp. mirin	**1 tsp. honey or barley**
1 Tbsp. tamari	**malt**

Pour over the sautéed vegetables and stir to mix. Rinse the eggplant well and pat dry. Add to the sauté, mix well, cover and let cook over medium heat until eggplant is tender (about 25 minutes).

Per serving: Calories: 204, Protein: 3 gm., Carbohydrates: 16 gm., Fat: 13 gm.

notes

marinated red peppers

See photo opposite page 81.

Yield: 2 cups
Prep: 2 hours

Preheat oven to 375°.

1. Place on a cookie sheet and bake for 40 minutes (until skins are shriveled):
   4 large red peppers
   Place hot peppers in a paper bag. Close tightly to let them steam until cooled, at least 45 minutes, placing bag on a plate to catch any leakage. Slip skins off, seed and cut cooled peppers in strips.

2. Place in a pint container and mix gently with:
   4 cloves garlic, minced
   ½ cup olive oil
   Cover and marinate overnight.

Per 2 Tbsp. serving: Calories: 129, Protein: 0 gm., Carbohydrates: 1 gm., Fat: 14 gm.

pasta shells in mushroom garlic sauce

Yield: 6 servings
Prep: 25 min.

1. Cook according to package directions:
   2 cups pasta shells

2. Sauté until mushrooms are tender:
   2 Tbsp. olive oil   **1 bunch scallions**
   1½ cups mushrooms,   **1 clove garlic, minced**
   chopped

3. Stir in until melted:
   3 Tbsp. garlic spread or
   3 Tbsp. butter or margerine mixed with
   ½ clove garlic, minced
   Whisk in until well blended:
   3 Tbsp. parmesan cheese

4. Combine shells in a large bowl with the sautéed vegetables and cheese. Add:
   ¼ cup parsley, chopped
   Serve immediately.

Per serving: Calories: 216, Protein: 5 gm., Carbohydrates: 23 gm., Fat: 9 gm.

stuffings

cornbread stuffing

Yield: 8 cups
Prep: 25 min.
Cook: 20 min.

Preheat oven to 350°.

1. Crumble into a large bowl:
    1 pan cornbread (pg.26)

2. Sauté over medium heat until tender, stirring frequently:
    2 Tbsp. olive oil   1 medium onion,
    2 sweet red peppers,   chopped
    chopped   2 cloves garlic, minced

3. In a food processor, puree until smooth:
    1½ cups toasted   3 Tbsp. olive oil
    pumpkin seeds   1 tsp. tamari
    ½ cup vegetable broth   ½ tsp. cayenne

4. Mix until well combined:
    the pumpkin seed puree   the crumbled cornbread
    the sautéed vegetables   ½ cup toasted pumpkin
        seeds
Spoon into an oiled baking dish and bake for 20 minutes.

Per 1 cup serving: Calories: 482, Protein: 16 gm., Carbohydrates: 33 gm., Fat: 18 gm.

wild rice stuffing

Yield: 6 cups
Prep: 45 min.

1. Place in a large pot and bring to a boil:
    1½ cups wehani rice,   1 vegetable bouillon cube
    washed   4½ cups water
    1 cup wild rice
Reduce heat, cover and simmer until water is absorbed (45 minutes). Turn into a large bowl.

2. Boil for 2 minutes:
    2 cups shallots
    water to cover
Drain, slip skins off shallots and quarter.

3. Sauté in a large frying pan over medium heat for 10 minutes:

3 Tbsp. olive oil	⅓ cup raisins
the shallots	¼ red wine or water
2 cloves garlic, minced	1 Tbsp. tarragon

4. Add the shallots and raisins to the rice with:

1 cup pine nuts
16 oz. plain yogurt

Stir until well mixed. Serve immediately.

Per 1 cup serving: Calories: 452, Protein: 15 gm., Carbohydrates: 55 gm.,
Fat: 19 gm.

fruited cous-cous stuffing

Yield: 8 cups
Prep: 20 min.
Bake: 30 min.

See photo, opposite page 80.

1. In a medium saucepan, bring to a boil over medium-high heat
and cook for 5 minutes:

2 cups water	1 cup prunes, pitted and
1 vegetable bouillon cube	coarsely chopped
	1 tsp. lemon rind, grated

2. Stir into the prune mixture:

2 cups cous-cous	½ tsp. cumin
½ tsp. cinnamon	½ tsp. black pepper

Remove from heat and let stand for 15 minutes.

3. While cous-cous is soaking, sauté in a frying pan over medium
heat until apples are almost soft (about 10 minutes):

2 medium apples, peeled,	2 medium onions,
cored and chopped into	chopped
½" chunks	2 Tbsp. sesame oil

4. Toss the prunes, apples and cous-cous in a large bowl until
well mixed with:

½ cup pine nuts, toasted

Preheat oven to 375°. Turn cous-cous into an oiled casserole
pan, cover with foil and bake for 20 minutes. Remove foil and
bake for 10 minutes more.

Per 1 cup serving: Calories: 290, Protein: 8 gm., Carbohydrates: 50 gm., Fat:
7 gm.

almond rice pilaf ☯

Yield: 4 servings
Prep: 1 hour

1. Sauté over medium-high heat in a large skillet:

 1 Tbsp. sesame oil   2 Tbsp. tamari
 2 cups mushrooms,
  sliced
 1 medium onion,
  chopped

2. When onions are tender (6-8 minutes) add and cook for 2 minutes:

 1½ cups brown rice

3. Add slowly:

 3 cups hot water or
  vegetable stock

Cover pan, reduce heat to low and simmer until liquid is absorbed (40-45 minutes).

4. Mix in:

 ½ cup almonds, toasted
  and chopped
 ½ cup raisins

Serve immediately.

Per serving: Calories: 351, Protein: 8 gm., Carbohydrates: 52 gm., Fat: 7 gm.

notes

apple-date stuffing

Yield: 8 cups
Prep: 30 min.
Bake: 40 min.

1. Sauté in a large skillet over medium-high heat until soft (about 15 minutes):

2 cups mushrooms, sliced
1 medium onion, chopped finely
4 stalks celery, chopped
2 cloves garlic

2 Tbsp. sesame oil
2 Tbsp. tamari
1 tsp. tarragon
1/2 tsp. sage

2. In a large bowl toss together:

4 cups whole wheat bread crumbs
2 tart apples, cubed
1 1/2 cups vegetable broth

1 cup pecans, toasted
1 cup dates, coarsely chopped

3. Preheat oven to 350°.

When the vegetables are tender add them to the bread crumb mixture and combine thoroughly. Spoon into a greased casserole dish, cover with foil and bake for 30 minutes. Uncover and bake 10 minutes longer.

Per serving: Calories: 416, Protein: 9 gm., Carbohydrates: 63 gm., Fat: 8 gm.

notes

main dishes

tofu

grilled tofu ☯ 78
marinated tofu with spicy peanut sauce 87
mock green fish 82
mock turkey en croute 88
mushroom-tofu stoganoff 79
sloppy joes 89
stuffed tofu cutlets with mushroom sauce . . 86
stuffed tofu in green sauce 84
tofu burgers 78
tofu loaf 78
tofu nut loaf 80
vegetarian lasagne 81

tempeh

curried tempeh wrap 92
spinach-tempeh quiche 90
tempeh with indonesian peanut sauce 91

beans

adzuki beans and vegetables ☯ 94
baked beans 94
chili 96
con queso rice 97
curried chick peas 99
enchilada bake 98
rice, beans and cheese casserole 93
saucy black beans 98

vegetables

broccoli and mushrooms with cashew sauce 105
greek eggplant pie 104
indian rice and vegetables 101
kasha with mushrooms 100
macro shepherd's pie ☯ 103
millet-mushroom pie 102
millet-vegie ragout 106
stuffed cabbage rolls with butternut sauce ☯ 106

cheese

pasta primavera 109
san bartelemao bake 108

tofu

grilled tofu ☯

Yield: 4 servings
Cook: 10 min.

1. Cut into ½" slices:
> 1 lb. tofu

2. Heat in a skillet:
> 2 Tbsp. sesame oil
> 1 tsp. toasted sesame oil

Fry tofu on both sides until golden (about 3 minutes on both sides). Drain on paper towels. Serve as main dish or use in a sandwich.

Per serving: Calories: 157, Protein: 9 gm., Carbohydrates: 4 gm., Fat: 13 gm.

tofu burgers

Yield: 4 servings
Prep: 30 min.

1. Combine in a medium bowl:
> 1 cup TVP
> ⅞ cup hot water

Soak for at least 15 minutes or until all water is absorbed.

2. In a large bowl mix,

> 1 lb. tofu, crumbled
> 1 cup carrot, grated
> ½ medium onion, minced

> 2 stalks celery, finely chopped
> 2 Tbsp tamari
> 1 Tbsp. seasoning mix

3. Combine the TVP and tofu mixtures and add:
> 2 eggs, beaten

Shape into patties and fry in a small amount of oil until golden (about 3 minutes per side). Drain on paper toweling and serve in buns with sliced tomatoes or pickles.

tofu loaf: Instead of patties, shape mix in an oiled loaf pan and bake for 45 minutes at 350°.

Per serving: Calories: 228, Protein: 26 gm., Carbohydrates: 17 gm., Fat: 9 gm.

mushroom-tofu stroganoff

Yield: 6 servings
Prep: 30 min.

1. Cook to al dente in a large pot with 2 quarts water:
   1 lb. noodles
   Drain and rinse.

2. Heat a large skillet and add:
   1 Tbsp. sesame oil   **2½ cups onions, thinly**
   3 cups mushrooms,   **sliced**
   sliced   **2 cloves garlic, minced**
   Sauté over medium high heat until onions are tender and
   mushrooms release their liquid (about 6-8 minutes).

3. Combine in food processor or blender and mix until smooth:
   ½ lb. tofu   **¼ cup cottage cheese**
   ¼ cup yogurt   **3 Tbsp. tamari**
   Combine noodles, mushrooms and onions and tofu mixture
   or serve sauce over the noodles.

variations: Sour cream can be used in place of yogurt and
cottage cheese. Poppy seeds sprinkled on top are a nice addition.

Per serving: Calories: 367, Protein: 20 gm., Carbohydrates: 61 gm., Fat: 5
gm.

notes

tofu nut loaf

Yield: 6 servings
Prep: 30-40 min.
Bake: 30 min.

1. Sauté in medium sauce pan until onions are tender, about 10 minutes:

1 Tbsp. sesame oil	1 large onion, chopped
1 cup mushrooms	1 sweet red or yellow
3 stalks celery, chopped	pepper
	2 cloves garlic, minced

2. While vegetable are cooking, mash in a large bowl:

2 lbs.tofu	2 tsp. sea salt
1 cup whole wheat flour	1 tsp. black pepper
1/3 cup TVP	1/2 tsp. tumeric
1/3 cup toasted sesame seeds	1/2 tsp. cumin
1/3 cup hazlenuts, chopped	

3. Blend in a small bowl with back of fork until well mixed:

1/3 cup tahini   3 Tbsp. white miso

4. Preheat oven to 350°. Combine the sautéed vegetables, tahini and miso with the tofu mixture and mix thoroughly. Spoon into loaf pan and bake for 30 minutes or until top is browned. Serve with Fig Sauce (pg. 62) or Mushroom Sauce (pg. 58).

variations: Form into patties and fry in just enough oil to keep from sticking. Drain on towels and serve in pita pockets with sprouts. Use almonds or walnuts instead of hazelnuts. For wheat-free diets use rice flour instead of whole wheat flour.

Per serving: Calories: 447, Protein: 25 gm., Carbohydrates: 32 gm., Fat: 27 gm.

fruited cous-cous stuffing, pg. 73

vegetarian lasagne

Yield: 6 servings
Prep: 40 min.
Baking: 45 min.

1. Have ready:

1 recipe for Italian
Tomato Sauce, pg. 58
½ lb. cheddar cheese,
shredded

¾ cup parmesan cheese

2. Cook in 4 quarts boiling water until al dente:

9 lasagne noodles

3. Combine in a food processor until smooth:

1 lb. tofu
⅓ cup parmesan cheese
1 Tbsp. parsley,
chopped

1 tsp. oregano
½ tsp. sea salt

4. Preheat oven to 350°. In a 9″ X 13″ pan cover bottom with a thin layer of tomato sauce, then 3 noodles, half of the tofu mixture, half the remaining sauce, 3 noodles, half the cheddar cheese, the other 3 noodles, the remaining sauce, and the rest of the cheddar and the parmesan cheese. Bake for 35 minutes. Let stand 10 minutes before serving.

Per serving: Calories: 507, Protein: 30 gm., Carbohydrates: 89 gm., Fat: 19 gm.

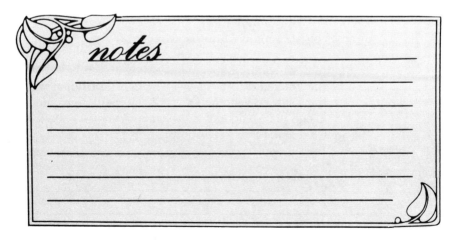

notes

Top: chili, pg. 96, Bottom: main meal sandwich, pg. 32, with marinated red peppers, pg. 71

mock green fish

Yield: 10 servings
Prep: 60 min.
Bake: 30 min.

1. For the marinade, puree in a blender for 1 minute:

½ cup white wine	2 Tbsp. mirin
½ cup red wine	2 Tbsp. white miso
½ cup tamari	2 Tbsp. grated ginger
½ small onion, minced	2 Tbsp. toasted sesame
2 cloves garlic, minced	oil

2. Split in half lengthwise:

5 lbs. firm tofu

Place in a deep bowl or 9" X 13" casserole pan. Pour over the marinade, cover and refrigerate several hours or overnight.

3. For the dressing, place in a covered saucepan:

1½ cups millet	**3 cups water**

Bring to a boil, reduce to a simmer and cook for 30 minutes. While millet cooks, sauté until tender:

2 Tbsp. toasted sesame oil	**1 cup mushrooms, sliced**
1 onion, chopped	**2 cloves garlic, minced**

Add:

⅓ cup red wine or sherry	**1 Tbsp. herb seasoning**
1 Tbsp. tamari	

Simmer covered for 10-15 minutes.

4. In a large bowl combine:

the cooked millet	**½ cup nutritional yeast**
the sautéed vegetables	**2 tsp. herb seasoning**
1 cup plain yogurt	

Mix well, set aside and keep warm.

notes

5. For the breading, mix together:

1 cup corn meal	1 tsp. tarragon
¼ cup whole wheat flour	½ tsp. sage
	½ tsp. black pepper

Drain the marinated tofu and coat with breading.

6. Heat in a skillet:

2-4 Tbsp. oil

Fry tofu slabs, turning when brown. You can also bake the tofu for 20 minutes in a 350° oven or broil for 6 minutes on a side, using less oil. When browned, lay out the tofu pieces side by side in two rows of five pieces each on a serving platter. Using a sharp knife, cut into the shape of a fish. Remove excess tofu pieces, chop and add to the millet dressing.

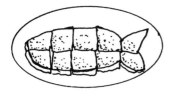

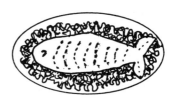

7. Have ready:

1 cup toasted almonds, slivered

Roll out:

1 package nori sheets

Cut each sheet to fit the top and sides of fish, leaving enough overlap to connect the pieces by wetting the edges with a little water. Use the toasted almond slivers for the eyes, gills and scales of the fish. Surround with parsley and fresh greens as a garnish.

8. For sauce, puree in a blender until smooth:

1½ cups water	1 inch piece fresh ginger root, cut up
⅓ cup white miso	2 Tbsp. tamari

Serve the millet dressing on the side and top with sauce. Return covered tofu to oven just to warm briefly.

Per serving: Calories: 664, Protein: 30 gm., Carbohydrates: 51 gm., Fat: 39 gm.

stuffed tofu in green sauce

Yield: 4 servings
Prep: 30 min. (Plus
      marinate overnight)
Cook: 15 min

1. For marinade, puree in a blender until smooth:

1 medium onion, chopped	2 tsp. sea salt
¼ cup red wine vinegar	1 tsp. cinnamon
5 Tbsp. peanut oil	½ tsp. cardamom powder
3 Tbsp. catsup	¼ tsp. black pepper
2 Tbsp. fennel seeds	20 whole peppercorns
2 Tbsp. cumin	8 whole cloves
2 tsp. ground cilantro	1" piece fresh ginger, grated

2. Slice off a 1" slab from each of:

    2 lbs. firm tofu

These will be used as the "tops". Make 4 cuts on the inside of the tofu block, leaving ½" sides. Scoop out the insides and crumble into a bowl. Cover and refrigerate. Cover the "tops" and blocks of tofu with the puree and marinate overnight.

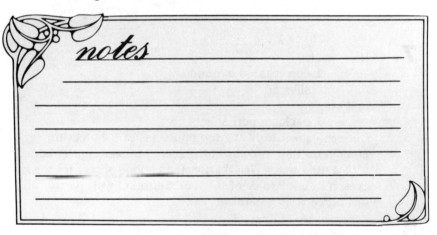

notes

3. For the sauce, puree in a blender until smooth:

½ small onion, chopped	2 cloves garlic
6 almonds, ground	1 sprig parsley
¼ cup bread crumbs	1½ cup vegetable broth
4 large romaine leaves, torn up	¼ cup sesame oil
	pinch cayenne

Set aside and keep warm.

4. Heat over medium-high heat in a medium skillet:
  2 Tbsp. sesame oil
Gently place the tofu blocks and tops in the pan and sauté until brown on all sides. Remove and keep warm.

5. Place in the skillet and sauté for 5 minutes:
  the reserved crumbled   **½ cup walnuts, chopped**
  tofu   **1 Tbsp. marinade**
Remove from heat and add:
  ¼ cup parsley

6. Stuff the tofu with the walnut-tofu mixture and replace the "top".

7. Toast over a gas flame or in a 350° oven until bright green:
  2 sheets nori
Slice the nori sheets in strips the width of the tofu blocks and long enough to wrap around it. Lay out the strips, place the tofu in the center and wrap the nori up and around. Lightly dampen the edges of the nori and secure them to each other.

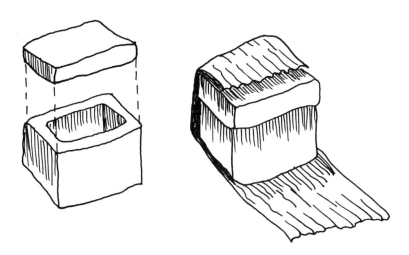

8. Spoon onto a plate just enough sauce to cover the bottom and place the tofu in the center. Garnish with parsley.

Per serving: Calories: 708, Protein: 24 gm., Carbohydrates: 20 gm., Fat: 58 gm.

stuffed tofu cutlets with mushroom sauce

Yield : 4 servings
Prep: 45 min. (Plus 1
hour marinating)
Bake: 35 min

1. For marinade, combine in a blender until well mixed:

½ medium onion,
chopped
½ cup tamari
½ cup white wine
3 Tbsp. white miso

3 Tbsp. rice vinegar
1 Tbsp. fresh ginger,
grated
2 cloves garlic, minced
2 cups water

Pour over:

2 lbs. tofu, cut into ½ lb. blocks

Refrigerate for at least 1 hour.

2. For stuffing, sauté over medium-high heat in the following order until onions are tender (6-8 minutes):

1 Tbsp. olive oil
½ cup onion, chopped
2 cloves garlic, minced

½ cup mushrooms,
sliced
3 Tbsp. tamari

Then add:

3 cups fresh bread
crumbs

1 tsp. basil
1 tsp. sage

3. Turn out stuffing mix into a large bowl and stir in:

1 cup celery, chopped   ½ cup carrot, grated

Set aside.

4. Remove tofu from marinade and cut out the centers from each block, like scooping out the centers of baked potatoes. Leave ¼″ sides and bottom. Crumble the scooped-out tofu into the stuffing mixture.

5. Preheat oven to 350°.
Mound the stuffing into each cutlet. Place in a baking pan and pour ¼ cup marinade over each cutlet. Cover with aluminum foil and bake for 30 minutes.
Remove foil and top with:

1 cup cheddar cheese, grated (opt.)

Continue baking until cheese is melted.

Per serving: Calories: 558, Protein: 31 gm., Carbohydrates: 76 gm., Fat: 13 gm.

marinated tofu with spicy peanut sauce

Yield: 4 servings
Prep: 30 min.
Bake: 30 min.

1. For marinade, blend:

½ cup tamari	1 clove garlic
½ inch fresh ginger root, grated	1 Tbsp. white miso

2. Cut into 1″ cubes:

1 lb. firm tofu

Cover with marinade and allow to sit at least 1 hour or overnight.

3. For sauce, sauté

1 medium onion, chopped	1 tsp. grated ginger root
1 clove garlic, minced	1 dried chili pepper, crushed

Blend in a blender or food processor:

2 cups hot water	½ cup peanut butter
1 cup unsweetened coconut, grated	1 Tbsp. tamari

Add to the onions. Stir well as it thickens.

4. Preheat oven to 350°. Place marinated tofu on a cookie sheet and bake for 35 minutes. Serve over brown rice topped with the peanut-coconut sauce.

variations: Instead of baking the marinated tofu, saute the cubes in oil until crisp and brown or steam in a steamer until soft and puffed.

Per serving: Calories: 367, Protein: 20 gm., Carbohydrates: 20 gm., Fat: 18 gm.

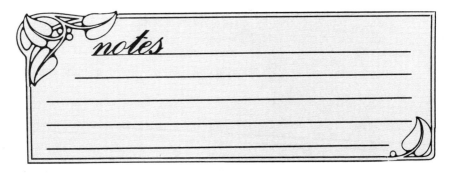

notes

mock turkey en croute

Yield: 6 servings
Prep: 60 min.
Cook: 30-40 min.

Preheat oven to 350°.

1. Sauté until mushrooms release their juices:

1 Tbsp. safflower oil	1 large onion, chopped
2 cups mushrooms, sliced	1 cup carrots, chopped

2. Add and then simmer for 10 minutes:

2 Tbsp. white wine	1 Tbsp. tamari
1 Tbsp. seasoning mix	8 oz. tempeh, cut into 1/4" pieces

3. Blend in a food processor until smooth:
   1/2 lb. tofu
   1 Tbsp. tamari

4. Grind until a fine meal:
   1/2 cup toasted almonds

5. Combine with the tempeh mixture and mix well:

tofu blend	8 oz. soy sausage or temeph
ground almonds	
1/2 cup nutritional yeast	1 tsp. garlic powder

Puree half of the mixture till smooth then add it back to the remaining mixture.
Preheat oven to 350°

6. Roll out 1/8" thick into 2 crusts:
   1 pkg. prepared pastry
   dough

Place on greased cookie sheet. Mold tempeh mixture on top of pastry. Cover with remaining pastry sheet and crimp edges. Bake until dough is golden. Philo pastry leaves can be used. Use a pastry brush to spread melted butter between 3 leaves for bottom crust and 3 leaves for top crust.

Per serving: Calories: 472, Protein: 22 gm., Carbohydrates: 31 gm., Fat: 20 gm.

sloppy joes

Yield: 6 servings
Prep: 20 min.
Cook: 35 min.

1. Sauté over medium heat until the onions are tender:

1 Tbsp. sesame oil	1 green pepper, chopped
1 medium onion, chopped	1 red pepper, chopped
	2 cloves garlic, minced

2. Add to the sautéed vegetables and mix well:

½ cup nutritional yeast	½ tsp. tumeric
1 tsp. dry mustard	½ tsp. cumin
¾ tsp. chili powder	⅛ tsp. black pepper

Sauté for 5 minutes more.

3. Combine with the vegetable mix:

1 lb. tofu, crumbled	2 large tomatoes, chopped
¾ cup TVP soaked in ¾ cup hot water	1-16 oz. can tomato puree
¼ cup molasses	2 Tbsp. cider vinegar

Reduce heat to low and simmer for about 20 minutes more. Adjust seasonings to taste. Serve over whole wheat hamburger buns.

Per serving: Calories: 234, Protein: 30 gm., Carbohydrates: 15 gm., Fat: 7 gm.

tempeh

spinach-tempeh quiche

Yield: 6 servings
Prep: 40 min.
Cook: 40 min.

1. For the crust, toss together with enough water to hold together:

> 2 cups whole wheat
>   bread crumbs
> ½ cup walnuts, chopped

Press into a 9″ pie plate.

2. Sauté

> 2 Tbsp. sesame oil
> 1 Tbsp. toasted sesame
>   oil
> 1 large onion, chopped
> 1 clove garlic, minced
> 1 Tbsp. tamari

When onions are soft, add:

> 1 lb. spinach, washed
>   and chopped
> 8 oz. tempeh, steamed
>   for 10 minutes and
>   cubed

Sauté for another 5 minutes. Spoon mixture into pie crust and sprinkle with:

> 1½ cups soy or jack
>   cheese, grated

Preheat oven to 400°.

3. Puree in a blender:

> 2 cups soy or low-fat   1 tsp. miso or prepared
>   milk   mustard
> 2 Tbsp. egg replacer

Pour into pie plate. Bake at 40 minutes or until custard has almost set. As it cools it will set up completely.

Per serving: Calories: 468, Protein: 26 gm., Carbohydrates: 41 gm., Fat: 20 gm.

tempeh with indonesian peanut sauce

Yield: 4 servings
Prep: 1 hour

The Dutch serve this sauce over "pommes frites" (fried potatoes) and it's also excellent served over brown rice and vegetables.

1. Combine in a 1 quart pan:

1 cup millet, rinsed	3 cups water

Cover, bring to a boil, reduce heat to low and simmer for 25-30 minutes, until water is absorbed.

2. In a covered pan, bring to a boil:

1 vegetable bouillon cube   1 cup water
or 1 tsp. vegetable
bouillon granules

Add:

½ lb. tempeh, thawed and cut into ½" cubes
Cover and simmer for 10 minutes.

3. In a medium skillet, heat:

2 tsp. peanut oil

Add:

1 medium onion,   1 tsp. fresh ginger,
  chopped   minced
2 cloves garlic, minced   ½ tsp. dried red pepper
3 dried chili peppers,   flakes (opt.)
  chopped

4. Combine in a blender:

½ cup unsweetened coconut
hot water to cover (⅓ cup)

Blend for 10 seconds. Place in the pan with onions and add:

1 cup peanut butter   2 Tbsp. tamari
¼ cup cider vinegar

Cook, stirring until peanut butter blends in. Add more water if necessary but sauce should be thick. Simmer for 15 minutes, stirring occasionally. Serve tempeh on the millet topped with the peanut sauce.

variation: Steam the tempeh cubes for 10 minutes, then sauté the cubes in a little peanut oil. Or omit the chili peppers for a milder sauce and add a pinch of sea salt.

Per serving: Calories: 581, Protein: 29 gm., Carbohydrates: 44 gm., Fat: 20 gm.

curried tempeh wrap

Yield: 4 servings
Prep: 30 min.
Cook: 1 hour

1. Sauté in a frying pan until tender:

2 Tbsp. sesame oil
1 medium onion, diced
2 cloves garlic, minced
3 dried red peppers, crushed
1 Tbsp. grated ginger

Allow to simmer for twenty minutes.

2. Add and mix well:

3 Tbsp. curry powder
1 Tbsp. tumeric
1½ tsp. ground coriander
1½ tsp. ground cumin

Continue to simmer for another 15 minutes until it is a thick paste.

3. For coconut milk, place in a blender:

1 cup fresh or dry
coconut, shredded
3 cups boiling water

Blend for 1 minute.

4. Pour into a sieve which has been placed over a one quart bowl. When cool, press and squeeze coconut until dry. This only keeps a few days, so freeze any unused milk.

5. Add to the curry mixture, stirring well:

1 cup vegetable stock
1½ cups coconut milk

6. Add one at a time to the pan:

½ lb. tempeh, steamed
and cubed
½ cup raisins
1 small cabbage, shredded

Allow to simmer for 50-60 minutes, stirring from time to time.

7. Remove from heat and add:

1 cup roasted cashews

Spoon onto a warm chapati and roll up (see pg. 28) or serve over hot rice. Serve immediately.

Per serving: Calories: 661, Protein: 22 gm., Carbohydrates: 47b gm., Fat: 23 gm.

beans

rice, beans and cheese casserole

Yield: 6 servings
Prep: 15 min.*
Cook: 30 min.

*Does not include cooking time for beans and rice.

1. Sauté until onion is tender:

1 Tbsp. safflower oil
2 medium onions,
   chopped

2 Tbsp. tamari

2. Preheat oven to 350°.
Combine in a large bowl:

2 cups brown rice,
   cooked
1½ cups navy beans,
   cooked
1½ cups pinto beans,
   cooked

1 cup sharp cheddar,
   grated
the sauteed onion
   mixture

3. Spread into an 8″ X 8″ baking pan and top with:

1 cup sharp cheddar,
   grated

Bake for 30 minutes.

Per serving: Calories: 369, Protein: 19 gm., Carbohydrates: 39 gm., Fat: 11 gm.

notes

baked beans

Yield: 6 servings
Prep: 15 min.
Baking: 30 min.

1. Sauté until onion is tender (about 5-8 minutes):

2 Tbsp. safflower oil
1 medium onion,
   chopped

2 cloves garlic, minced

Preheat oven to 350°.

2. Mix in a large bowl with sautéed onion until well combined:

5 cups navy beans,
   cooked
1 cup tomato puree
¼ cup molasses

1 Tbsp. tamari
1 tsp. dry mustard
1 tsp. chili powder

3. Pour into a casserole dish, cover and bake for 30 minutes.

Per serving: Calories: 289, Protein: 13 gm., Carbohydrates: 48 gm., Fat: 5 gm.

adzuki beans and vegetables

Yield: 4 servings
Prep: 1½ hours

1. In a covered pot cook until tender (about 1 hour):

1 cup adzuki beans,
   rinsed

2″ piece kombu (sea
   vegetable)
4 cups water

2. While beans are cooking, combine in a 1 quart covered pot:

1 cup brown rice
1¾ cups water

pinch sea salt

Bring to a boil, cover, reduce heat to low and simmer for about 40 minutes or until all water is absorbed.

3. Combine in a bowl:

½ cup dried arame
8 shitake mushrooms

Rinse three times with fresh water. Remove tough mushroom stems and slice mushrooms.

4. Sauté in a medium pan over medium-high heat until soft:

    1 tsp. toasted sesame oil   1 medium onion,
    2 tsp. sesame oil   chopped
                              1 Tbsp. tamari

Add the mushrooms and arame.

5. Steam until crisp-tender:

    1 cup broccoli   1 cup carrots, chopped
    1 cup cauliflower

6. Combine in a blender, adding the water slowly:

    ½ cup tahini (roasted)   2 Tbsp. rice vinegar
    ¼ cup white miso   ½ cup water
    2 Tbsp. mirin

Sauce should be smooth and thick.

7. On each plate place rice, top with beans, mushrooms and steamed vegetables. Spoon tahini sauce over the top. Sprinkle with gomazio, if desired, and serve immediately.

Per serving: Calories: 477, Protein: 17 gm., Carbohydrates: 50 gm., Fat: 44 gm.

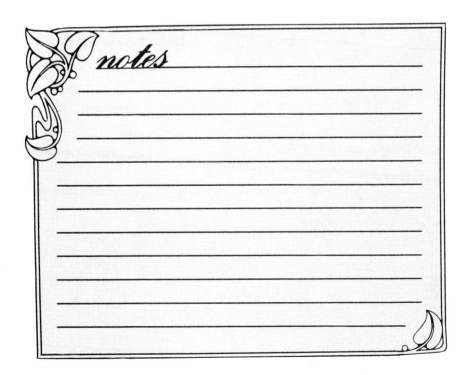

notes

chili

Yield: 8 servings
Prep: 30 min.
Cook: 30 min.

See photo opposite page 81.

1. Sauté in a large soup pot over medium-high heat until peppers are limp:

2 Tbsp. sesame oil	1 large red pepper,
1 large onion, chopped	chopped
1 large green pepper,	2 cloves garlic, minced
chopped	

Stir frequently and add:
5 large tomatoes,
chopped

2. Stir in until well combined:

3 Tbsp. tamari	1 tsp. ginger
2 tsp. cumin	1 tsp. tarragon
2 tsp. cayenne (opt.)	1 tsp. basil

Bring to a simmer and cook over medium-high heat for about 5 minutes.

3. Add:

2 cups kidney beans,	8 oz. soy sausage,
cooked	crumbled
1 cup raw corn	16 oz. tomato puree
1 can black olives,	
chopped	

Combine thoroughly and lower heat to medium-low. Simmer for at least 30 minutes, stirring occasionally. Serve with corn bread.

Per serving: Calories: 304, Protein: 11 gm., Carbohydrates: 29 gm., Fat: 21 gm.

notes

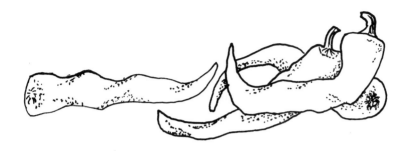

con queso rice

Yield: 4 servings
Prep: 30 min.*
Bake: 30 min.

*Does not include cooking time for rice and beans.

1. Have ready:
2 cups cooked brown rice
1 cup cooked black
beans

2. Sauté until tender:
2 Tbsp. oil
1 medium onion,
chopped

¼ cup green chili pep-
pers, chopped
3 cloves garlic, minced

3. Combine in a bowl:
2 cups cheddar cheese,
grated
8 oz. cottage cheese
Reserve 1 cup of cheese mixture for a topping.

4. Preheat oven to 350°. Combine rice, beans and sautéed
vegetables in a large bowl. Layer with the cheese mixture in a
8″ X 8″ casserole dish, ending with the rice layer. Bake for 30
minutes. Remove, top with rest of cheese, return to oven for
the last 10 minutes.

Per serving: Calories: 492, Protein: 26 gm., Carbohydrates: 33 gm., Fat: 22
gm.

enchilada bake

Yield: 6 servings
Prep: 40 min.
Baking: 55 min.

1. Have ready:
   1 recipe for Chili, pg. 96   12 corn tortillas
   2 cups cheddar cheese,
      shredded
Preheat oven to 350°.

2. Blend together in a blender or food processor to make a "mock sour cream":
   1½ cups cottage cheese
   1½ cups plain yogurt

3. Ladle over the bottom of a 9″ X 13″ pan:
   1 cup chili
Place 6 tortillas over the chili, allowing them to overlap.

4. Spoon half of the remaining chili on top of the tortillas, top with half the "sour cream", half the cheddar cheese and repeat, starting with 6 more tortillas and ending with the cheese. Bake for 45 minutes. Let stand 10 minutes before serving.

Per serving: Calories: 773, Protein: 36 gm., Carbohydrates: 71 gm., Fat: 40 gm.

saucy black beans

Yield: 2 cups
Prep: 15 min.

1. Sauté until tender:
   2 Tbsp. olive oil   ½ medium onion,
   1 clove garlic, minced   chopped

2. Combine in a food processor and puree:
   2 cups black beans,   1 Tbsp. ginger, grated
      cooked and ½ cup   1 Tbsp. tamari
      liquid
   2 Tbsp. apple cider
      vinegar or rice vinegar

3. Add to the food processor and continue pureeing until smooth:

> **sautéed onion mixture**

Serve over sautéed peppers and rice.

Per serving: Calories: 155, Protein: 6 gm., Carbohydrates: 18 gm., Fat: 8 gm.

curried chick peas

Yield: 4 servings
Prep: 25 min.
Cook: 1½ hrs

1. Cook until tender (about 1½ hours):

4 cups water	**½ tsp. ginger**
1 cup chick peas (soaked overnight)	**1 bay leaf**

Drain.

2. Sauté over medium heat until tender:

2 Tbsp. sesame oil	**1 Tbsp. fresh ginger, grated**
1 medium onion, chopped	**1 tsp. sea salt (optional)**
2 cloves garlic, minced	

3. Add to onion mixture:

1 cup coconut milk, pg. 92	**the chickpeas**
1 Tbsp. curry powder	

Reduce heat and simmer, stirring to combine.

4. Add together:

> **1 Tbsp. arrowroot**
> **½ cup cooking broth**

Return to the pan and simmer until thickened (about 5 minutes). Serve over brown rice.

Per serving: Calories: 419, Protein: 13 gm., Carbohydrates: 39 gm., Fat: 15 gm.

vegetables

kasha with mushrooms

Yield: 4 servings
Prep: 15 min.
Cook: 35 min.

1. Combine in a bowl with a wire whisk:

1 egg, beaten
1 cup roasted buckwheat
kernels (kasha)

Stir to coat kasha thoroughly. Pour into a frying pan and cook over medium heat, stirring constantly as it toasts, 4 to 5 minutes.

2. Bring to a boil:

2 cups water or
vegetable stock

Carefully add to kasha, lower heat, cover and simmer until liquid is absorbed.

3. Sauté for 10 minutes or until onions are tender:

2 Tbsp. safflower oil   **1 medium onion,**
1 cup mushrooms, sliced   **chopped**
                                 sea salt and pepper to
                                 taste

Toss with cooked kasha and serve immediately.

Per serving: Calories: 192, Protein: 6 gm., Carbohydrates: 24 gm., Fat: 8 gm.

notes

indian rice and vegetables

Yield: 6 servings
Prep: 30 min.
Cooking: 1 hour

1. Heat a large heavy pan that has a tight fitting lid. Add:
>   **2 Tbsp. sesame oil**
>   **1 yellow onion, thinly**
>   **sliced**

Stir fry 5 minutes, then add:
>   **2 cups uncooked long**
>   **grain brown rice**

Stir fry 5 minutes more, then add:
>   **4 cups water**   **1 tsp. sea salt**
>   **1 tsp. tumeric**   **¼ tsp. black pepper**

Bring to a boil, mix well and cover the pan. Reduce heat and simmer for 30 minutes.

2. Prepare 2 cups of fresh vegetables, such as:
>   **mushrooms, sliced**   **broccoli, broken into ½ "**
>   **green beans, cut in thin**   **flowerettes**
>   **diagonals**   **celery, sliced thinly on**
>   **cauliflower, broken into**   **the diagonal**
>   **½" flowerettes**

3. Add the vegetables to the rice and cover pan. Continue to cook 15 minutes until all liquid is absorbed. Remove from heat, let stand for 10 minutes.

Roast at 300° for 10 minutes:
>   **½ cup almonds or**
>   **cashews, chopped**

Turn rice and vegetables onto a serving platter. Top with roasted, chopped nuts.

Per serving: Calories: 252, Protein: 6 gm., Carbohydrates: 32 gm., Fat: 7 gm.

millet-mushroom pie

Yield: 4-6 servings
Prep: 35 min.
Cook: 30 min.

1. Bring to boil in a pot:
> **1 cup millet, rinsed**
> **2 cups water**

Reduce heat to low and simmer until all water is absorbed, about 25-30 minutes.

2. Heat in a skillet:
> **2 Tbsp. sesame oil**

Add and cook until tender:
> **1 medium onion,**
> **chopped**

Stir in:
> **1 cup mushrooms,**   **2 Tbsp. tamari**
> **chopped**   **1 tsp. seasoning mix**
> **½ cup white wine or**
> **water**

Cook on medium-low heat for 15 minutes, stirring occasionally.
Preheat oven to 375°.

3. Combine in a large bowl and mix well:
> **8 oz. plain yogurt**   **the millet**
> **⅓ cup nutritional yeast**   **the sautéed vegetables**

4. Spoon into a lightly greased 9″ pie plate and top with:
> **½ cup walnut halves**

Bake for 30 minutes.

variation: Add ¼ cup of beet juice for a lovely red color!

Per serving: Calories: 261, Protein: 7 gm., Carbohydrates: 24 gm., Fat: 14 gm.

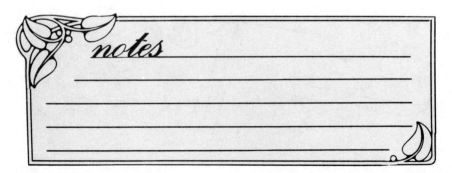

notes

macro shepherd's pie ☯

Yield: 8 servings
Prep: 1½ hours
Bake: 35 min.

Preheat oven to 375°.

1. Prepare batter according to directions:
**½ Cornbread recipe,
        pg. 26**
Oil a 9″ X 13″ casserole dish and pour in batter. Bake for 20 minutes. Turn oven down to 350° after cornbread is removed.

2. In a large skillet, sauté until tender:
**1 Tbsp. sesame oil
1 medium onion, chopped**

Add and cook another 3 minutes:
2 cups cauliflower
Stir in and bring to a boil:
**2 cups millet, rinsed   2 Tbsp. tamari
4½ cups water**
Reduce heat, cover and simmer until water is absorbed, about 20 minutes.

3. While millet is cooking, sauté in another pan until crisp-tender:
**1 Tbsp. sesame oil   1 cup cabbage, shredded
1 cup mushrooms. sliced   ½ cup carrots, sliced
1 cup broccoli   1 medium onion,
                            chopped**
Set aside.

4. Grate and set aside:
2 cups soy or jack cheese or mochi

5. Place the cooked millet and cauliflower in a food processor and puree until smooth.

6. Layer on the baked cornbread crust half the grated cheese, the sautéed vegetables, the remaining cheese and the pureed millet. Top with:
sesame seeds
Bake for 35 minutes.

Per serving: Calories: 276, Protein: 11 gm., Carbohydrates: 20 gm., Fat: 15 gm.

greek eggplant pie

Yield: 6 servings
Prep: 1 hour
Cook: 40 min.

1. For pie crust, measure into small bowl:

    **2 cups whole wheat
pastry flour**

Make a well in the flour and slowly pour in:

    **½ cup oil
¼ cup hot water**

Stir just enough to mix. Form into 2 balls, cover with a damp cloth and set aside.

2. Puree in a food processor until smooth:

½ cup feta cheese or tofu	**1 cup skim milk**
	1 Tbsp. olive oil
½ cup walnuts, toasted	**¼ tsp. cayenne**

3. Sauté until tender:

2 Tbsp. olive oil	**2 cloves garlic, minced**
1 large onion, chopped	

Add:

2 medium eggplant, chopped	**1 tsp. dill**
4 cups tomatoes, chopped	**1 tsp. thyme**
	1 tsp. rosemary
2 cups zucchini, chopped	**1 tsp. sea salt**

Simmer for at least ½ hour.

4. Puree in a food processor until smooth:

2 cups cooked garbanzo beans	**¼ cup tahini**
	¼ cup lemon juice
½ cup cooking liquid	
3 cloves garlic, minced	

Preheat oven to 375°. Roll out each ball of pie crust dough to fit a 8″ X 8″ casserole dish. Line bottom and sides of the casserole with one half of the rolled dough. Mix the blended beans with the sautéed vegetables and pour into casserole. Top with feta spread and pie crust dough. Slash crust.

Bake for 35-40 minutes or until bubbly.

Per serving: Calories: 703, Protein: 21 gm., Carbohydrates: 66 gm., Fat: 45 gm.

broccoli and mushrooms with cashew sauce

Yield: 4 servings
Prep: 45 min.

1. Combine in a 1 quart pan:
>   **1 cup brown rice, rinsed**
>   **2 cups water**

Bring to a boil, cover, reduce heat to low and cook until liquid is absorbed (30-35 minutes).

2. Sauté in a large skillet over medium-high heat:
>   **1 Tbsp. sesame oil**   **1 medium onion,**
>   **1 cup mushrooms, sliced**   **chopped**
>   **2 Tbsp. tamari**

Coarsely chop:
>   **1 lb. broccoli**

When onions are soft, add broccoli, sauté 5-6 minutes. Reduce heat, cover pan, cook 5 minutes more.

3. Puree in a blender:
>   **1 cup cashews, toasted**   **1¹/₂ cups water**
>   **¹/₄ cup tamari**

To serve, spoon rice onto plates, cover with vegetables and top with sauce.

Per serving: Calories: 376, Protein: 14 gm., Carbohydrates: 40 gm., Fat: 8 gm.

millet-vegie ragout

Yield: 6 servings
Prep: 40 min.

1. In a 2 quart pan combine:
> **2 cups millet, rinsed**
> **5 cups water**

Bring to a boil, reduce heat to low, cover pan and simmer 15 minutes.

2. Add to millet:

> **¼ cup safflower oil**
> **¼ cup tamari**
> **5 small red potatoes, quartered**
> **2 cloves garlic, minced**
> **2 stalks celery, chopped**

> **1 medium carrot, chopped**
> **1 large onion, chopped**
> **1 tsp. rosemary**
> **¼ tsp. sage**
> **¼ tsp. tarragon**

Cover pan, continue cooking until vegetables are tender (20-25 minutes). Serve with crusty bread and a green salad.

Per serving: Calories: 268, Protein: 6 gm., Carbohydrates: 39 gm., Fat: 10 gm.

stuffed cabbage rolls with butternut sauce ☯

Yield: 4 servings
Prep: 1 hour

1. Have ready:
> **3 cups brown rice, cooked**
> **1 medium butternut squash, steamed**

2. Steam until tender:
> **8 large cabbage leaves**

Set aside.

3. Combine in a medium bowl:

    1 cup shitake
    mushrooms
    ½ cup arame

Rinse, cover with water and allow to soak 10 to 15 minutes. Drain and reserve liquid.

4. Sauté until tender:

2 tsp. sesame oil	**1 medium onion,**
1 tsp. toasted sesame oil	**chopped**

Add:

    ½ cup mushrooms,
    sliced
    3 Tbsp. tamari

Cover and simmer for 10 minutes. Add the sliced shitake mushrooms and arame. Cook five more minutes.

5. Combine the brown rice in a medium bowl with the onions, mushrooms, arame and cooking liquid. Cut the core from each cabbage leaf, spoon on mixture, turn in sides and roll the leaf going away from your body. Set aside, keep warm.

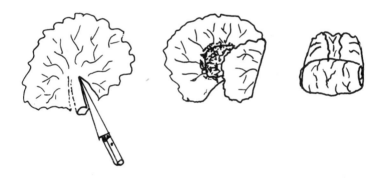

6. Scoop the pulp from the butternut squash. Place in a food processor and puree until smooth with:

2 Tbsp. rice vinegar or	**1 Tbsp. white miso**
lemon juice	**1 Tbsp. mirin**

Use enough of the soaking water from the arame and mushrooms to create a sauce-like consistency.

7. Spoon sauce onto plate and place cabbage roll in center. Sprinkle with gomazio, if desired, and serve immediately.

Per serving: Calories: 327, Protein: 8 gm., Carbohydrates: 67 gm., Fat: 4 gm.

cheese

san bartelemao bake

Yield: 6 servings
Prep: 40 min.
Bake: 40 min.

1. Sauté until tender:
    2 Tbsp. olive oil   1 clove garlic, minced
    1 onion, chopped

2. Add, cover pan and simmer until almost tender:
    1 large head cauliflower   ½ cup white wine
    in pieces

3. Puree in a blender or food processor:
    1 lb. ricotta cheese   1 lb. cottage cheese

4. Broil until brown and slightly scorched:
    2 large red peppers
You can also place the peppers on a cookie sheet and bake
in a hot oven for 45 minutes. When cooked, place in a brown
bag on a plate or cookie sheet and close tightly, allowing
them to steam until cool. Remove and peel the skin off. Seed
and cut into strips.

5. Have ready:
    3 cups cooked pasta   1 package soy bacon
    (corn pasta if available)   strips
    1 cup fontini cheese or
    mozzarella, grated
Preheat oven to 350°. Toss the vegetables, cheese, peppers and
pasta together in a large bowl. Spoon into a casserole dish
and top with layers of the grated cheese and bacon strips.
Bake for 40 minutes.

Per serving: Calories: 505, Protein: 30 gm.,
Carbohydrates: 30 gm., Fat: 19 gm.

pasta primavera

Yield: 4 servings
Prep: 20 min.
Cook: 20 min.

1. Sauté the following vegetables in a medium frying pan, adding them one at a time and only cooking them slightly or al dente:

2 Tbsp. sesame oil	2 yellow squash, julienned
2 medium carrots, julienned	2 cloves garlic, minced
1 red pepper, julienned	1 oz. dried shitake mushrooms, soaked and sliced

2. Add:

1 cup heavy cream	1/4 cup fresh dill, chopped
1/2 cup parmesan cheese, grated	salt and pepper to taste

3. Cook in water until al dente:
1-12 oz. package egg
noodles

Drain and place in a large bowl. Pour sauce and vegetables over noodles and toss until thoroughly coated. Serve immediately.

Per serving: Calories: 617, Protein: 20 gm., Carbohydrates: 63 gm., Fat: 24 gm.

notes

desserts

cakes

carrot cake 114
coconut carrot cake 114
german carob cake 112
holiday fruit cake 113
lemon mousse trifle 113
orange hazelnut cake 114
peach crisp 115

cheesecakes

banana-carob cheesecake 116
basic cheesecake 116
carob-yogurt cheesecake 117

pies

butternut pie 121
creamy pumpkin pie 120
gran american apple pie 118
mock mincemeat pie 119

cookies and bars

apricot squares 124
carob chip brownies 126
carob mousse tartlettes 124
date nut bars 122
doo daas 123
energy bars 122
maple-almond cookies ☯ 123
roasted almond cookies ☯ 128
tofu-lava 127

puddings and fruit

carob-mint parfait 130
coconut-pineapple kanten 132
desert whip 129
glazed pears 131
lemon mousse 129
raita 132
tofu fruit whip 130

icings & toppings

almond whipped cream 133
apricot glaze 135
carob-cream cheese icing 134
carob fudge icing 134
carob-ricotta frosting 134
coconut date icing 133
ricotta cream cheese spread 135
whipped topping 133

desserts

Barley malt or Yinnie (rice) syrup can be used as a replacement for honey or maple syrup. Sesame, safflower or corn oil can be used for baking purposes.

cakes

german carob cake

Yield: 16 servings
(three 9″ layers)
Prep: 20 min.
Bake: 40 min.

Preheat oven to 350°. Grease and flour 3 round 9″ cake pans.

1. Combine in a large bowl:

3 cups apple juice
1 cup honey or barley malt
½ cup sesame or corn oil

2 tsp. vanilla
3 eggs or 2 Tbsp. egg replacer

2. Combine in another bowl:

2 cups whole wheat pastry flour
2 cups unbleached flour
1 cup toasted carob powder*

1 tsp. baking soda
1 tsp. baking powder
1 tsp. sea salt

*Carob powder can be toasted on a pie plate in a 350° oven about 10 minutes.

Stir the dry ingredients one cup at a time into the wet ingredients

3. Pour in batter filling pans ¾ way full. Bake for 40 minutes or until knife inserted in center comes out clean.

4. When done remove cake from oven and allow to cool. Remove from pans and either split each layer in half making six layers or leave whole for three. Frost each layer with Coconut-Date Icing (pg. 133).

Per serving: Calories: 277, Protein: 5 gm., Carbohydrates: 51 gm., Fat: 8 gm.

gran american apple pie, pg. 118

lemon mousse trifle

See photo opposite page 113.

Yield: 12 servings
Prep: 20 min.

1. Have ready:
Lemon Mousse, pg. 129   4 kiwi fruit, sliced
²/₃ cup coconut, toasted

2. Slice thinly:
1-16 oz. pound cake

3. Line the bottom of a large bowl with slices of pound cake. Spoon in half the mousse, then layer with the pound cake, kiwi fruit, coconut, other half of mousse, some sliced kiwi, and a coconut design on top.

4. Chill.

Per serving: Calories: 435, Protein: 11 gm., Carbohydrates: 50 gm., Fat: 6 gm.

holiday fruit cake

Yield: 12-14 servings
(1 bundt cake)
Prep: 30 min.
Bake: 1 hour

Preheat oven to 350°.

1. Blend with an electric beater:
1 stick butter, softened   5 eggs
½ cup fructose   1 tsp. vanilla
Set aside.

2. Sift together in a large bowl:
2 cups whole wheat flour   1 tsp. nutmeg
1 tsp. baking soda   1 tsp. cinnamon
1 tsp. baking powder   ½ tsp. sea salt
1 tsp. ground cloves

3. Combine both mixtures together along with:
2 cups assorted dried fruits and nuts, chopped
(dates, apricots, figs, walnuts, pecans, etc.)

Pour into buttered, floured bundt pan and bake for 1 hour. Top with Apricot Glaze (pg. 135).

Per serving: Calories: 341, Protein: 8 gm., Carbohydrates: 47 gm., Fat: 11 gm.

lemon mousse trifle (this page)

carrot cake

Yield: 2 loaves or 24 cup cakes
Prep: 30 min.
Bake: 40-50 min.

1. Toss together and set aside:

    3 cups grated carrots   1 cup walnuts, chopped
    1 cup raisins

2. Sift together in a large bowl:

    2 cups rice flour   1½ tsp. baking soda
    2 cups rye flour   1½ tsp. baking powder
    2 tsp. cinnamon

Set aside. Preheat oven to 350°.

3. Mix together until well combined:

    3 cups apple juice   1½ Tbsp. egg replacer or
    ¾ cup honey   2 eggs
    ¼ cup oil   1 tsp. vanilla

4. Pour this into the flour mixture and stir until just mixed. Then fold in the carrot mixture and mix well. Batter should be thick. Spoon into well oiled muffin tins or loaf pans—be sure to fill the muffins tins. Bake cupcakes for 40 minutes—2 loaves for 50 minutes (or until a knife inserted in the center comes out clean).

coconut carrot cake: Add ¾ cup coconut in with the grated carrot mixture.

Per serving: Calories: 211, Protein: 3 gm., Carbohydrates: 37 gm., Fat: 5 gm.

orange hazelnut cake

Yield: 12-14 servings
(1 bundt cake or
two 9″ layers)
Prep: 30 min.
Bake: 40 min.

Preheat oven to 350°. Grease and lightly flour a bundt pan or two 9″ round cake pans.

1. Sift together into a large bowl:

    2 cups whole wheat   ¼ cup carob powder
      pastry flour   1½ tsp. baking powder
    2 cups unbleached white   1½ tsp. baking soda
      flour

2. Mix together until well blended:

2 eggs	½ cup butter, softened
1 cup low-fat or soy milk	12 oz. apple juice
½ cup orange juice	concentrate
	granted rind of 1 orange

Add to dry ingredients and mix until well blended.

3. Add to the batter and mix in:

1 cup hazelnuts, chopped
fine

Pour batter into bundt pan or cake pans. Bake for 40 minutes or until toothpick inserted comes out clean. Ice with Carob-Cream Cheese Frosting (pg. 134) or a marmalade glaze.

Per serving: Calories: 309, Protein: 7 gm., Carbohydrates: 39 gm., Fat: 6 gm.

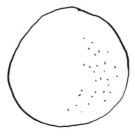 

peach crisp

Yield: 4-6 servings
Prep: 40 min.
Bake: 35 min.

Preheat oven to 350°.

1. Combine in a saucepan, bring to a boil:

1 lb. ripe peaches, peeled	1 cup raisins
and cut up	1 Tbsp. agar-agar flakes
1 cup apple juice	

Lower heat and simmer for 15 minutes.

2. Place in a food processor:

2 cups Granola, pg. 20

With on/off pulses add until just moistened.:

2 Tbsp. water

Press half of granola mixture into the bottom of an 8" X 8" baking pan. Pour peaches into dish and sprinkle remaining granola on top. Bake for 35 minutes.

Per serving: Calories: 384, Protein: 8 gm., Carbohydrates: 65 gm., Fat: 10 gm.

cheesecakes

See **Tips for Blending Tofu**, page 129.

basic cheesecake

Yield: 8-10 servings
     (one 9″ round pan)
Prep: 30 min.
Bake: 1½ hour

1. Combine:

> 3 cups unsweetened
> cookie crumbs
> 2 Tbsp. water

Press into a 9″ spring form pan. Set aside. Preheat oven to 350°.

2. Combine in a food processor and puree until smooth:

> 2 lbs. soft tofu
> ½ cup barley malt
> 1 cup apple juice
> concentrate

> 1 cup almonds, finely
> ground
> 1 tsp. vanilla
> juice of 1 lemon

Pour into crust and bake for 1½ hours or until toothpick inserted in center comes out clean. Cool.

Top with apricot jam or fruit in season. Decorate with toasted whole almonds.

Per serving: Calories: 330, Protein: 13 gm., Carbohydrates: 36 gm., Fat: 8 gm.

banana carob cheesecake

Yield: 8 servings
     (one 8″ round pan)
Prep: 15 min.
Bake: 1 hour

1. Mix together:

> 1 cup muesli cereal
> 2-3 Tbsp. apple juice concentrate (enough
> to make it stick together)

Press into the bottom of a well-greased 8″ spring form pan. Set aside. Preheat oven to 350°.

2. Combine in a blender or food processor until smooth and creamy:

> 2 ripe bananas
> 1½ lbs. soft tofu
> ½ cup apple juice
> concentrate

> 1 Tbsp. egg replacer
> 1 tsp. vanilla
> juice of 1 lemon

3. With the processor running, add gradually until well blended:

    1 cup carob powder

4. Stop the machine and fold in, using a rubber scraper:

    1 cup unsweetened
    carob chips

Pour into the spring form pan and bake for 1 hour or until the center is firm. Cool before slicing.

Per serving: Calories: 381, Protein: 13 gm., Carbohydrates: 55 gm., Fat: 15 gm.

carob-yogurt cheesecake

Yield: 8 servings
(one 8″ round pan)

Preheat oven to 325°.

Prep: 30 min.
Bake: 1½ hours

1. Mix together:

    1½ cups carob cookie   **2 tsp. water**
    crumbs

Press into the bottom of a buttered 8″ spring form pan. Set aside.

2. Puree in a food processor until smooth:

    24 oz. low fat cottage   **2 tsp. vanilla**
    cheese   **1 tsp. cinnamon**
    ½ cup fructose
    ½ cup plain yogurt

3. Stir in:

    1 cup carob chips

Pour into cake pan.

4. Place a shallow pan of water on bottom oven rack. Place cheesecake on middle rack and bake 1½ hours. Turn off heat and let cake cool in oven with door ajar. Slice when completely cool. Can be iced with Carob-Ricotta Frosting (pg. 134).

Per serving: Calories: 359, Protein: 27 gm., Carbohydrates: 39 gm., Fat: 10 gm.

pies

gran american apple pie

Yield: 6-8 servings (one
9″ pie)
Prep: 40 min.
Bake: 30 min.

See photo opposite page 112.

1. Combine in a saucepan:

5 large tart apples,
peeled and sliced
1 cup apple juice
½ cup raisins
¼ cup lemon juice

¼ cup honey
1 tsp. nutmeg
1 tsp. allspice

Bring to a boil, reduce heat and simmer until apples are tender (about 15 minutes).

2. Remove ½ cup of cooking liquid and whisk in:

1 Tbsp. arrowroot

Return liquid to saucepan and stir to combine. Set aside.
Preheat oven to 375°.

3. In a food processor combine to a coarse meal:

2 cups walnuts
1 tsp. butter

Reserve ½ cup of nut mixture to use as a topping for the pie.
Add to processor:

¾ cup shredded sharp
cheddar cheese

Blend briefly just to combine. Press mixture into an ungreased pie plate to form a crust. Do not press over lip of plate as the cheese will melt over the side.

4. Pour apple mixture into pie shell, top with remaining nut mixture and bake for 30 minutes.

variations: Substitute ½ cup apple juice concentrate or ¼ cup maple syrup for the honey.

Per serving: Calories: 427, Protein: 11 gm., Carbohydrates: 28 gm., Fat: 21 gm.

mock mincemeat pie

Yield: 6-8 servings (one
9″ pie)
Prep: 10 min.
Bake: 30 min.

1. For filling, combine in a saucepan, cover, and bring to a boil:

1½ cups raisins ⅔ cup apple juice
1 cup chopped apples juice of 1 orange
1 cup dried apricots, grated rind of 1 orange
unsulphured, minced

Reduce heat to low and simmer for 15 minutes.

2. Remove pan from heat and stir in:

½ cup honey ½ tsp. cinnamon
¼ cup crushed soda ½ tsp. ground cloves
crackers

Set aside. Preheat oven to 350°.

3. For crust, combine in a food processor:

1½ cups pecans ¼ cup butter or
½ cup coconut margarine

Blend until it resembles coarse meal. Press half of the nut mixture into a lightly oiled 9″ pie plate and spoon in the fruit filling. Top with the rest of the nut mixture and bake for 30 minutes.

Per serving: Calories: 493, Protein: 5 gm., Carbohydrates: 70 gm., Fat: 11 gm.

notes

creamy pumpkin pie

Yield: 6-8 servings (one
9″ pie)
Prep: 35 min.
Bake: 40 min.

1. Split into quarters, remove seeds, place in a steamer basket
and steam until tender:
1 medium pumpkin
Allow to cool slightly, scoop out the pulp into a food
processor.

2. Add to the food processor:

16 oz. skim ricotta cheese	**3 Tbsp. arrowroot**
½ cup honey or barley malt	**1 tsp. cinnamon**
	½ tsp. nutmeg
	¼ tsp. cloves

Puree until smooth. Preheat oven to 375°.

3. Combine with your hands in a separate bowl:

½ cups pecans, chopped	**¼ cup butter or**
1 cup coconut	**margarine**

Press mixture into a lightly greased 9″ pie plate.

4. Pour the pumpkin filling into the pie crust and bake for 40
minutes.

Per serving: Calories: 405, Protein: 11 gm., Carbohydrates: 38 gm., Fat: 15
gm.

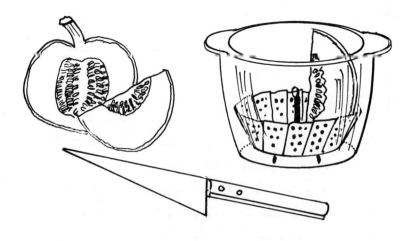

_____
_____
_____
_____
_____
_____
_____
_____
_____

butternut pie

Yield: 6-8 servings (one
9" pie)
Prep: 30 min.
Bake: 30 min.

1. Prepare crust by mixing in a medium bowl:

    ¾ cup Granola (pg. 20)   **2 Tbsp. water**
    ¼ cup coconut

Press into a 9" pie plate. Set aside.

2. Cook 2 medium butternut squash (or 4 medium delicatta squash) by halving them, scooping out the seeds, inverting the halves in a steamer basket and steaming until tender (about 20 minutes) until a knife passes through the outer shell easily. Scoop the pulp out into a food processor when cool enough to handle. Preheat oven to 350°.

3. Add in with the squash and blend until smooth:

    ½ cup honey or barley   **1 tsp. cinnamon**
    malt   **1 tsp. vanilla**
    2 Tbsp. arrowroot

Pour into the prepared pie crust and bake for 30 minutes. Serve with Whipped Topping (pg. 133) or Almond Whipped Cream (Pg. 133).

Per serving: Calories: 303, Protein: 6 gm., Carbohydrates: 65 gm., Fat: 3 gm.

cookies & bars

energy bars

Yield: 24 2"x 4" bars
Prep: 10 min. (plus
chilling time)

1. Mix in a large bowl with your hands:

1¾ cups peanut butter
¾ cup honey
½ cup unsweetened
carob chips
½ cup shredded coconut

½ cup granola
½ cup raisins
½ cup crispy rice cereal

2. Make sure everything is well mixed. Turn into a 9" x 13" baking dish and flatten out as evenly as possible. Cover and chill for at least one hour. Cut into bars. Chill.

Per serving: Calories: 183, Protein: 5 gm., Carbohydrates: 20 gm., Fat: 6 gm.

date nut bars

Yield: 18 bars
Prep: 20 min.
Bake: 35 minutes

Preheat oven to 375°.

1. Combine in a large bowl:

1 cup pitted dates,
chopped
2 cups unsweetened
coconut

2 cups chopped walnuts
1½ cups unsweetened
carob chips

Set aside.

2. Puree in a blender until smooth:

1 lb. tofu
1 cup chopped dates

1 cup apple juice

Add fruit mixture and mix thoroughly. Fold into 13" X 9" casserole pan (glass). Top with extra carob chips or walnuts. Bake for 35 minutes. Remove from oven and allow to cool before slicing.

Per bar: Calories: 232, Protein: 22 gm., Carbohydrates: 29 gm., Fat: 11 gm.

doo daas

Yield: 18 2" bars
Prep: 30 min.
Bake: 15 min.

Preheat oven to 350°.

1. Melt in the top of a double boiler:
3 cups unsweetened carob chips

Add half way through melting process:
½ cup apple juice concentrate or barley malt

Remove from heat.

2. Fold in until thoroughly mixed:
1 cup unsweetened coconut
¾ cup walnuts, chopped
Spread onto cookie sheet and bake for 15-20 minutes. Cut into 2" bars while still warm.

Per bar: Calories: 203, Protein: 3 gm., Carbohydrates: 20 gm., Fat: 12 gm.

maple-almond cookies

Yield: 3 dozen
Prep: 15 min.
Bake: 12-15 min.

1. Mix together in a large bowl:
1½ cups whole wheat flour
1½ cups rolled oats (finely ground in processor)
1½ cups finely ground almonds
1 tsp. sea salt
1 tsp. cinnamon
Set aside.

2. Whisk together in a separate bowl:
¾ cup maple syrup
½ cup corn oil or safflower oil
2 tsp. vanilla
Add to dry ingredients. Mix thoroughly.

3. Preheat oven to 350°. Form small balls of dough and make indentations in the center of each, using your thumb. Place on a greased cookie sheet and fill with raspberry fruit preserves. Bake for 12-15 minutes.

Per cookie: Calories: 119, Protein: 3 gm., Carbohydrates: 13 gm., Fat: 5 gm.

apricot squares

Yield: 9 squares
Prep: 20 min.
Bake: 30 min.

1. Place in a saucepan:

    3 cups dried apricots   3 cups apple juice
    (unsulphured), chopped
    coarsely

Bring to a boil, reduce heat to low and simmer covered for 20 to 30 minutes; stir occasionally so they don't stick to the pan.

2. Preheat oven to 350°. Mix together:

    1 cup walnuts, chopped   ¼ cup butter or
    ½ cup rolled oats   margarine, softened
                                1 tsp. cinnamon

3. Spoon apricots evenly into a lightly oiled 8″ X 8″ baking pan and top with above mixture, pressing down lightly into the apricots. Bake for 30 minutes. Cut into 9 squares.

Per square: Calories: 305, Protein: 7 gm., Carbohydrates: 41 gm., Fat: 10 gm.

carob mousse tartlettes

Yield: 12 tartlettes
Prep: 40 min.

1. Toast by spreading on a pie plate and baking at 350° for around 10 minutes:

    ¾ carob powder

2. For the mousse filling, combine in a food processor until smooth:

    16 oz. skim ricotta   ¾ cup fructose
    cheese   1 tsp. vanilla
    8 oz. vanilla yogurt
    the toasted carob powder

Spoon into a bowl.

3. Whip until they form stiff peaks:

    4 egg whites

Fold whites into filling mixture.

4. Fold in:

    ½ cup hazelnuts, roasted, chopped fine

Chill. Preheat oven to 425°.

5. For the tart shells, mix until smooth:

²/₃ cup fructose	¹/₂ tsp. vanilla
¹/₂ cup unbleached flour	2 egg whites
4 Tbsp. butter, melted	1 egg

This will make a thin batter. On a greased cookie sheet, spoon ¼ cup of the batter onto the cookie sheet for each cookie, swirling the batter with the back of a spoon to make a 4″ cookie. Repeat until there are 6 cookies on a sheet. Bake for 6-8 minutes, until the edges brown 1″ into the cookie. Meanwhile, assemble 6 small jars (1½″-2″ diameter) upside-down. Cut 5″ diameter heavy duty aluminum foil circles. When cookies are done, quickly remove them from the oven and drape them over the jars. Shape the foil over the cookies to form fluted edges. Allow to cool while the second batch is in the oven. When cool, spoon carob mousse filling into tartlettes and serve.

Per tartlette: Calories: 281, Protein: 8 gm., Carbohydrates: 36 gm., Fat: 7 gm.

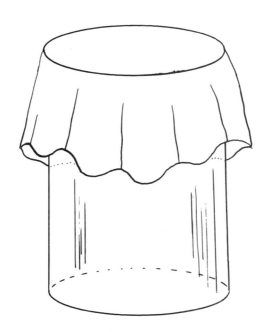

carob chip brownies

Yield: 16 2" brownies
Prep: 20 min.
Bake: 20-25 min.

Preheat oven to 350°.

1. Sift together in small mixing bowl and set aside:

> 1 cup unbleached flour   ¼ tsp. sea salt
> 1 tsp. baking powder

2. Cream together:

> ½ cup butter or
>   margarine, softened
> ¼ cup carob powder

Then add:

> 2 eggs, slightly beaten   1 tsp. vanilla
> ½ cup maple syrup

Mix thoroughly. Add to flour and mix well.

3. Stir in:

> ½ cup carob chips
> ½ cup walnuts, chopped

Pour batter into a buttered 8" x 8" pan and bake for 20-25 minutes.

Per brownie: Calories: 167, Protein: 3 gm., Carbohydrates: 177 gm., Fat: 8 gm.

notes

tofu-lava

Yield: 9 servings
Prep: 40 min.
Bake: 35 min.

This is a version of
Middle Eastern baklava.

1. Combine in a saucepan, cover and slowly bring to a boil:

3 cups apples, peeled,	**½ cup raisins**
cored and chopped	**½ cup apple juice**

Reduce heat and simmer until apples are tender (about 15 minutes). You may add a little water if necessary to keep apples from scorching until they make their own juice.

2. Combine:

1½ cups walnuts,	**1 tsp. cinnamon**
chopped	
2 tsp. butter or	
margarine	

It should resemble coarse meal. Set aside.

3. Puree in food processor until smooth:

½ lb. tofu	**1 Tbsp. lemon juice**
½ cup barley malt or	**1 tsp. vanilla**
maple syrup	

Set aside. Preheat oven to 375°.

4. Have ready:

½ lb. phyllo dough
6 Tbsp. butter or
margarine, melted

Lightly brush two sheets of phyllo with melted butter. Layer the sheets on top of each other and fold in half, then fold in half again. Place in the bottom of an oiled 8″ X 8″ baking pan. Be sure to keep the remaining sheets of phyllo covered with a damp towel to keep them from drying. Spoon onto the dough half of the apple mixture, add another layer of two buttered and folded sheets of phyllo, half of the tofu, half of the walnuts, and repeat layers ending with phyllo. Bake for 35 minutes. Can be served hot or cold.

Per serving: Calories: 407, Protein: 9 gm., Carbohydrates: 46 gm., Fat: 18 gm.

roasted almond cookies

Yield: 32 2″ squares
Prep: 15 min.
Bake: 40 min.

Preheat oven to 350°.

1. Combine in a large bowl:

4 cups brown rice flour
3 cups almonds (roasted, chopped small)
2 cups raisins
1½ cups sesame seeds (roasted)

1 cup rolled oats
1 Tbsp. orange rind (opt.)
2 tsp. cinnamon
½ tsp. sea salt

Set aside.

2. In a large saucepan heat until well dissolved:

1½ cups apple juice
¾ cup tahini

½ cup barley malt (or honey)
1 tsp. vanilla

Pour this warm liquid over the dry ingredients and mix well.
Spread onto cookie sheet with sides, using a rolling pin to
spread and smooth evenly. Bake 20-30 minutes until firm.

3. Remove from pan and spread the top with:

1 cup raspberry fruit preserves

Slice into bars and serve cooled.

Per bar: Calories: 346, Protein: 8 gm., Carbohydrates: 47 gm., Fat: 11 gm.

notes

puddings & fruit

tips for blending tofu

Not all food processors are powerful enough to blend tofu smoothly for puddings or pie fillings. If you plan on using a blender, crumble the tofu in a bowl and whisk in the other ingredients. Blend the mixture in several batches, combining the batches thoroughly when you are finished.

lemon mousse

Yield: 6 servings
Prep: 15 min.

1. Puree in a food processor or blender until smooth:

2 lbs. soft tofu	**2 tsp. tumeric**
¾ cup maple syrup	**juice of 2 lemons**
1 Tbsp. vanilla extract	**grated rind of 2 lemons**
2 tsp. lemon extract	

2. Chill. Serve garnished with fresh strawberries or use in Lemon Mousse Trifle (pg. 113).

Per serving: Calories: 212, Protein: 12 gm., Carbohydrates: 29 gm., Fat: 6 gm.

desert whip

Yield: 6 servings
Prep: 45 min.
Chill: 1 hour

1. Soak in warm water for 45 minutes:

1 cup figs
1 cup dates

Drain.

2. In a blender or food processor, puree the figs and dates until smooth with:

1 lb. soft tofu	**½ cup apple juice**
½ cup toasted carob powder	**concentrate**

Chill.

Per serving: Calories: 236, Protein: 8 gm., Carbohydrates: 53 gm., Fat: 1 gm.

tofu fruit whip

Yield: 2 cups
Prep: 15 min.

1. Place in a blender or food processor and puree until smooth:

1 large, ripe banana	¼ cup apple juice
½ lb. soft tofu	concentrate
½ pint strawberries	¼ cup honey (optional)
½ cup raisins	1 tsp. vanilla
	¼ tsp. cinnamon

2. Spoon into dessert dishes or use as a topping.

Per ½ cup serving: Calories: 149, Protein: 6 gm., Carbohydrates: 29 gm., Fat: 3 gm.

carob-mint parfait

Yield: 4 servings
Prep: 10 min.(plus chill-ing time)

1. Have ready:

1 recipe Whipped Topping, pg. 133

2. Puree in a food processor or blender until very smooth:

1 lb. soft tofu	⅛ cup lemon juice
½ cup carob powder	1 Tbsp. vanilla
¼ cup honey	1 tsp. mint extract

Chill.

3. Layer in 4 parfait glasses: carob mousse, sliced strawberries, Whipped Topping, repeat and top with a whole strawberry.

Per serving: Calories: 176, Protein: 10 gm., Carbohydrates: 33 gm., Fat: 5 gm.

glazed pears

Yield: 4 servings
Prep: 20 min.
Bake: 40 min.

Preheat oven to 350°.

1. Peel and core from the bottom leaving the stem intact:
4 medium pears
Slice just across the bottom of each pear to make a flat surface so pear stands upright. Place in a glass baking dish.

2. Combine in a small bowl:

⅔ cup apricot preserves	**1 Tbsp. lemon peel**
⅓ cup apple juice concentrate	**juice of 1 lemon**
	⅓ cup white wine

Spoon a couple of tablespoons of glaze over each pear and bake for 40 minutes, continuing to spoon glaze over pears at about 12 minute intervals until done. Remove onto individual serving plates.

3. Combine in a small bowl:

½ cup Almond Cookie crumbs (pg. 123) or coconut macaroon crumbs	**¼ cup toasted almonds, finely ground**

Use as a garnish and sprinkle on each pear.

Per serving: Calories: 467, Protein: 4 gm., Carbohydrates: 90 gm., Fat: 5 gm.

notes

coconut-pineapple kanten

Yield: 4 servings
Prep: 15 min.
Chill: 2 hours

1. Pour into saucepan and heat until it boils:
  3 cups coconut-pineapple
  juice

2. Shred into small pieces and add to the juice:
  1 10″ bar agar agar or 6
  Tbsp. agar flakes
Reduce heat to medium low and simmer until agar is fully dissolved. Pour into a mold or glass dish and refrigerate 1 hour.

3. Remove kanten from refrigerator and fold in thoroughly:
  ½ cup chopped
  pineapple
  ½ cup shredded coconut
Return to the refrigerator until set (1 hour).

Per serving: Calories: 155, Protein: 1 gm., Carbohydrates: 31 gm., Fat: 4 gm.

raita

Yield: 2 servings
Prep: 10 min.

1. Prepare and place in serving bowls:
  1 cup mixed fruit of choice, chopped
  (apples, pears, grapes, blueberries,
  peaches, plums, cherries, apricots, etc.)

2. Mix together:
  1 pint plain yogurt   **½ tsp. nutmeg**
  ½ tsp. cinnamon
Add to the fruit and toss gently. Garnish with fresh mint leaves and serve well chilled.

Per serving: Calories: 180, Protein: 8 gm., Carbohydrates: 21 gm., Fat: 5 gm.

icings & toppings

whipped topping

Yield: 1½ cups
Prep: 10 min.

1. Combine in a blender or food processor until smooth:

1 lb. soft tofu	**1 Tbsp. lemon juice**
¼ cup soy milk	**1 tsp. vanilla**
¼ cup maple syrup	

2. Chill.

Per 2 Tbsp. serving: Calories: 47, Protein: 3 gm., Carbohydrates: 5 gm., Fat: 2 gm.

almond whipped cream

Yield: 1¼ cups
Prep: 10 min.

1. Puree in a food processor or blender until very smooth:

1 lb. soft tofu	**1 tsp. vanilla**
½ cup toasted almonds	**1 tsp. lemon juice**
3 Tbsp. honey	

2. Chill. Serve on fresh fruit.

Per 2 Tbsp. serving: Calories: 95, Protein: 5 gm., Carbohydrates: 8 gm., Fat: 3 gm.

coconut date icing

Yield: 5 cups
Prep: 15 min.

1. Puree in a food processor until smooth:

3 cups bahri dates, pitted	**1 cup coconut milk,**
2 cups walnuts, chopped fine	**pg. 92**
	1 cup unsweetened,
1 cup tahini	**grated coconut**
	1 tsp. vanilla

Spread over anything!

Per ¼ cup serving: Calories: 248, Protein: 6 gm., Carbohydrates: 14 gm., Fat: 25 gm.

carob fudge icing

Yield: 2½ cups
Prep: 20 min. (plus cool-
ing time)

1. Melt in the top of a double boiler:
>   **2 cups unsweetened
>   carob chips
>   ½ cup apple juice
>   concentrate**

2. Puree in a blender:
>   **8 oz. low-fat cottage
>   cheese**

When carob chips are melted, add the cottage cheese and
mix thoroughly. Allow to cool before frosting a cake.

Per ¼ cup serving: Calories: 222, Protein: 8 gm., Carbohydrates: 25 gm.,
Fat: 10 gm.

carob-ricotta frosting

Yield: 1 cup
Prep: 10 min.

1. Blend in a food processor until smooth:
>   **8 oz. low fat ricotta**   **⅛ cup fructose**
>   **cheese
>   ½ cup carob powder**

Per ¼ cup serving: Calories: 158, Protein: 8 gm., Carbohydrates: 21 gm.,
Fat: 6 gm.

carob-cream cheese icing

Yield: 1½ cups
Prep: 15 min.

1. Combine in a food processor until smooth:
>   **8 oz. low fat cottage**   **2 Tbsp. honey**
>   **cheese**   **1 tsp. vanilla**
>   **8 oz. cream cheese,
>   softened
>   ¼ cup carob powder**

Per ¼ cup serving: Calories: 217, Protein: 13 gm., Carbohydrates: 13 gm.,
Fat: 10 gm.

ricotta cream cheese spread

Yield: 2 cups
Prep: 10 min.

1. Cream together until smooth:
>   1 cup ricotta cheese   ½ cup apple juice
>   1 cup cream cheese,   concentrate
>   softened   1 tsp. vanilla

Great over carrot cake or zucchini bread.

Per ¼ cup serving: Calories: 168, Protein: 8 gm., Carbohydrates: 5 gm., Fat: 9 gm.

apricot glaze

Yield: 2 cups
Prep: 5 min.

1. Place in saucepan with enough apple juice to cover:
>   2 cups dried,
>   unsulphered, apricots

2. Bring to a boil, cover and reduce heat and simmer until soft, about 30 minutes. Puree in a food processor until smooth. Spoon over Holiday Fruit Cake, pg. 113.

Per ¼ cup serving: Calories: 125, Protein: 2 gm., Carbohydrates: 32 gm., Fat: 0 gm.

notes

beverages

yogurt smoothie

Yield: 2 cups

1. Blend together in a blender until smooth:

  1 cup frozen fruit **¾ cup apple juice**
  chunks (banana,   **2 heaping Tbsp. yogurt,**
  apple, grape,   **any flavor**
  strawberries)

More fruit will yield a thicker shake, if you prefer.

Per 1 cup serving: Calories: 76, Protein: 1 gm., Carbohydrates: 17 gm., Fat: 1 gm.

banana date nut smoothie

Yield: 2 cups

1. Blend together in a blender until smooth:

  1 cup apple juice or **3 pitted dates**
  coconut milk (pg. 92) **¼ cup pecans**
  2 bananas, frozen

Per 1 cup serving: Calories: 293, Protein: 3 gm., Carbohydrates: 53 gm., Fat: 3 gm.

tropical smoothie

Yield: 2 cups

1. Blend together in a blender until smooth:

  1 cup apple juice **3 pitted dates**
  1 cup frozen tropical
  fruit (pineapple,
  banana, papaya,
  mango)

Per 1 cup serving: Calories: 133, Protein: 1 gm., Carbohydrates: 34 gm., Fat: 0 gm.

carob-peanut butter smoothie

Yield: 2 cups

1. Blend together in a blender until smooth:

1 cup apple juice
2 large frozen bananas

2 heaping Tbsp. peanut butter
1 heaping Tbsp. carob powder

Per 1 cup serving: Calories: 306, Protein: 7 gm., Carbohydrates: 56 gm., Fat: 5 gm.

papaya-carob malt shake

Yield: 2 cups

1. Blend together in a blender until smooth:

1 cup papaya juice
¾ cup carob-malt soy milk
¼ lb. soft tofu

1 large frozen banana
1 tsp. carob protein powder

Per 1 cup serving: Calories: 303, Protein: 9 gm., Carbohydrates: 52 gm., Fat: 8 gm.

protein shake

Yield: 2 cups

1. Blend together in a blender until smooth:

1 cup skim milk
½ frozen banana
3 Tbsp. soy powder

3 Tbsp. skim milk powder (non-instant)
1 Tbsp. peanut butter

Per 1 cup serving: Calories: 190, Protein: 21 gm., Carbohydrates: 18 gm., Fat: 2 gm.

strawberry flip

Yield: 2 cups

1. Blend together in a blender until smooth:

1 cup skim milk
1 cup fresh strawberries

1 tsp. honey

Per 1 cup serving: Calories: 78, Protein: 5 gm., Carbohydrates: 14 gm., Fat: 1 gm.

measures & equivalents

US standard measures

3 teaspoons = 1 tablespoon
4 tablespoons = ¼ cup
5 ⅓ tablespoons = ⅓ cup
16 tablespoons = 1 cup
1 cup = 8 fluid ounces
4 cups = 1 quart
4 quarts = 1 gallon

approximate metric equivalents

1 ounce = 28 gm.
1 pound = 454 gm.
1 teaspoon = 5 ml.
1 tablespoon = 15 ml.
1 fluid ounce = 30 ml.
1 cup = 240 mi.
1 quart = 950 ml.
1 gallon = 3.8 l.

some helpful substitutions

milk

Soy milk can be substituted for regular or skim milk in any recipe. In place of 1 cup of milk, use 1 cup water with ½ tsp. baking soda and 1 Tbsp. lemon juice or vinegar. Almonds or cashews pureed in water, then put through a sieve or cheesecloth, also make good milk substitutes.

butter

1 cup butter = ⅞ cup oil + ½ tsp. sea salt

egg

For body and binding properties: apple/fruit sauce, cottage cheese, nut butter or tofu are good replacements for eggs.
For rising power: 1 tsp. baking powder per egg
For binding: Use 1 tsp. egg replacer (made from potato starch and tapioca) plus 2 Tbsp. water per egg.

About the nutritional analyses:

Recipe ingredients not included in the analyses are those such as garnishes, serving suggestions and variations. If the recipe serves 4 to 6, the analysis is averaged out to 5 servings. If a certain amount of one or more foods is called for, the first food is included in the analysis.

index

Adzuki Beans and Vegetables, 94
Agar-agar, 10
Almond Cookies, Roasted, 128
Almond Pate, Tempeh, 36
Almond Rice Pilaf, 74
Almond Whipped Cream, 133
Almondine, Mock Chicken, 44
Apple Pie, Gran American, 118
Apple-Date Stuffing, 75
Apricot Glaze, 135
Apricot Squares, 124
Arame, 10
Arrowroot, 10
Avocado Soup, Cool, 50
Baba Ganouj, 37
Baked Beans, 94
Banana Date Nut Smoothie, 136
Banana-Carob Cheesecake, 116
Barley, Soup, Mushroom; 55
Bars, Date Nut, 122
Bars, Energy, 122
Basic Bread, 28
Basic Cheesecake, 116
Bean Tostada, 31
Beans and Cheese Casserole,
    Rice, 93
Beans, Adzuki and Vegetables, 94
Beans, Baked, 94
Beans, cooking, 13
Beans, Saucy Black, 98
Biscuits, Pumpkin, 23
Biscuits, Whole Wheat Drop, 24
Black Beans, Saucy, 98
Blueberry Wheat Cakes, 21
Braised Chestnuts & Brussels
    Sprouts, 66
Bread, Basic, 28
Bread, Zucchini, 26
Brie, Croissant with, 30
Broccoli and Mushrooms with
    Cashew Sauce, 105
Brownies, Carob Chip, 126
Brussels Sprouts, Braised
    Chestnuts &, 66
Burgers, Tofu, 78
Buttermilk Wheat Cakes, 21
Butternut Pie, 121
Butternut Sauce, Stuffed Cabbage
    Rolls with, 106
Butternut Squash, Stuffed, 67
Cabbage Rolls with Butternut Sauce,
    Stuffed, 106
Cake, Carrot, 114
Cake, Coconut Carrot, 114
Cake, German Carob, 112

Cake, Holiday Fruit, 113
Cake, Orange Hazelnut, 114
California Salad, 47
Cardamom Carrots, 66
Carob, 10
Carob Cake, German, 112
Carob Chip Brownies, 126
Carob Fudge Icing, 134
Carob Malt Shake, Papaya; 137
Carob Mousse Tartlettes, 124
Carob-Cream Cheese Icing, 134
Carob-Mint Parfait, 130
Carob-Peanut Butter Smoothie, 137
Carob-Ricotta Frosting, 134
Carob-Yogurt Cheesecake, 117
Carrot Cake, 114
Carrot Cake, Coconut, 114
Carrot-Yogurt Soup, 56
Carrots, Cardamom, 66
Cashew Sauce, Broccoli and
    Mushrooms with, 105
Cereal with Stewed Plums, Rice, 22
Chapatis, Whole Wheat, 28
Cheese Casserole, Rice,
    Beans and, 93
Cheese Dip, Garlic-Dill, 34
Cheese, Herbed Yogurt, 35
Cheesecake, Banana-Carob, 116
Cheesecake, Basic, 116
Cheesecake, Carob-Yogurt, 117
Chestnuts & Brussels Sprouts,
    Braised, 66
Chick Peas, Curried, 99
Chili, 96
Chutney, Fruit, 63
Chutney, Mango, 63
Coconut Carrot Cake, 114
Coconut Date Icing, 133
Coconut-Pineapple Kanten, 132
Con Queso Rice, 97
Cookies, Roasted Almond, 128
Cooking terms, 17
Cool Avocado Soup, 50
Cornbread, 26
Cornbread Stuffing, 72
Cornbread, Herbed Tofu, 27
Cous-Cous Stuffing, Fruited, 73
Cranberry Orange Nut Bread, 25
Cranberry Sauce, 61
Cream Cheese Icing, Carob; 135
Cream Cheese Pitas, 29
Cream Cheese Spread, Ricotta, 135
Creamed Spinach, 68
Creamy Pumpkin Pie, 120
Crisp, Peach, 115
Croissant with Brie, 30
Curried Chick Peas, 99

Curried Split Pea Soup, 51
Curried Tempeh Wrap, 92
Cutlets with Mushroom Sauce,
  Stuffed Tofu, 86
Daikon, 10
Daikon Slaw, 40
Date Icing, Coconut, 133
Date Nut Bars, 122
Date Nut Smoothie, Banana, 136
Desert Whip, 129
Dip, Garlic-Dill Cheese, 34
Dip, Tofu, 35
Doo Daas, 123
Dressing, Miso, 42
Dried Fruit Jam, 64
Drop Biscuits, Whole Wheat, 24
Eggplant Pie, Greek, 104
Eggplant, Hot Garlic, 70
Enchilada Bake, 98
Energy Bars, 122
Falafel in Pita, 30
Fig Sauce, 62
Fruit Cake, Holiday, 113
Fruit Chutney, 63
Fruit Jam, Dried, 64
Fruit Relish, Onion, 64
Fruit Sauce, 62
Fruit Soup, 51
Fruit Whip, Tofu, 130
Fruited Cous-Cous Stuffing, 73
Fudge Icing, Carob, 135
Garlic Eggplant, Hot, 70
Garlic-Dill Cheese Dip, 34
German Carob Cake, 112
Glaze, Apricot, 135
Glazed Pears, 131
Gomazio, 10
Grain Salad with Yogurt Dressing,
  Mixed, 43
Grains, cooking, 13
Gran American Apple Pie, 118
Granola Deluxe, 20
Greek Eggplant Pie, 104
Green Fish, Mock, 82
Green Sauce, 59
Grilled Tofu, 78
Hazelnut Cake, Orange, 114
Hearty Tomato Sauce, 58
Herbed Tofu Cornbread, 27
Herbed Yogurt Cheese, 35
Holiday Fruit Cake, 113
Hot Garlic Eggplant, 70
Humble Miso Soup, 52
Hummus, 34
Icing, Carob Fudge, 135
Icing, Carob-Cream Cheese, 135
Icing, Coconut Date, 133

Indian Rice and Vegetables, 101
Indonesian Peanut Sauce,
  Tempeh with, 91
Italian Pasta Salad, 48
Italian Tomato Sauce, 58
Jam, Dried Fruit, 64
Kanten, Coconut-Pineapple, 132
Kasha with Mushrooms, 100
Kombu, 10
Land & Sea Vegetable Soup, 53
Lasagne, Vegetarian, 81
Lemon Mousse, 129
Lemon Mousse Trifle, 113
Lo-Cal Mock Sour Cream, 59
Loaf, Tofu, 78
Loaf, Tofu Nut, 80
Macro Shepherd's Pie, 103
Macrobiotics, 12
Main Meal Sandwich, 32
Mango Chutney, 63
Maple Nut Millet, 20
Maple-Almond Cookies, 123
Marinated Red Peppers, 71
Marinated Tofu with Spicy
  Peanut Sauce, 87
Mayonnaise, Tofu, 40
Meat substitutes, 6
Menu planning, 6-7
Millet, Maple Nut, 20
Millet-Mushroom Pie, 102
Millet-Vegie Ragout, 106
Mint Parfait, Carob, 130
Mirin, 10
Miso, 10
Miso Dressing, 42
Miso Dressing, Sprout Salad with,
40
Miso Soup, Humble, 52
Miso Wakame Soup, 52
Miso-Pesto Sauce, 60
Miso-Tahini Sauce, 60
Mixed Grain Salad with Yogurt
  Dressing, 43
Mochi, 10
Mock Chicken Almondine, 44
Mock Chicken Salad, 44
Mock Green Fish, 82
Mock Mincemeat Pie, 119
Mock Sour Cream, Lo-Cal, 59
Mock Tuna, 45
Mock Turkey en Croute, 88
Mousse Tartlettes, Carob, 124
Mousse Trifle, Lemon, 113
Mousse, Lemon, 129
Muesli cereal, 10
Muffins, Tea, 24

Mushroom Garlic Sauce, Pasta
  Shells in, 71
Mushroom Pie, Millet; 102
Mushroom Sauce, 58
Mushroom Sauce, Stuffed Tofu
  Cutlets with, 86
Mushroom-Barley Soup, 55
Mushroom-Tofu Stoganoff, 79
Mushrooms with Cashew Sauce,
  Broccoli and, 105
Mushrooms, Kasha with, 100
Nori, 10
Nut Bars, Date, 122
Nut Bread, Cranberry Orange, 25
Nut Loaf, Tofu, 80
Nut Puree, Tofu, 37
Nutritional yeast, 10
Nuts and seeds, toasting, 15
Onion-Fruit Relish, 64
Orange Hazelnut Cake, 114
Orange Nut Bread, Cranberry, 25
Orange Sesame Sauce, 60
Papaya-Carob Malt Shake, 137
Parfait, Carob-Mint, 130
Pasta Primavera, 109
Pasta Salad, Italian, 48
Pasta Salad, Rainbow, 48
Pasta Shells in Mushroom
  Garlic Sauce, 71
Pate, Tempeh Almond, 36
Pate, Vegetable, 36
Pea Soup, Spicy, 51
Peach Crisp, 115
Peanut Butter Smoothie, Carob; 137
Peanut Sauce, Marinated Tofu
  with Spicy, 87
Peanut Sauce, Tempeh with
  Indonesian, 91
Peanut Soup, Spicy Tomato; 54
Pears, Glazed, 131
Pesto Sauce, Miso; 60
Pie, Butternut, 121
Pie, Creamy Pumpkin, 120
Pie, Gran American Apple, 118
Pie, Greek Eggplant, 104
Pie, Macro Shepherd's, 103
Pie, Millet-Mushroom, 102
Pie, Mock Mincemeat, 119
Pilaf, Almond Rice, 74
Pineapple Kanten, Coconut, 132
Pita, Falafel in, 30
Pitas, Cream Cheese, 29
Potato Salad, Sunflower, 41
Potatoes Boulangere, 69
Protein requirements, 6
Protein Shake, 137
Pumkin Pie, Creamy, 120
Pumpkin Biscuits, 23

Pumpkin Soup, 54
Quiche, Spinach-Tempeh, 90
Ragout, Millet-Vegie, 106
Rainbow Pasta Salad, 48
Raita, 132
Red Peppers, Marinated, 71
Relish, Onion-Fruit, 64
Reuben, Unclassical, 31
Rice and Vegetables, Indian, 101
Rice Cereal with Stewed Plums, 22
Rice Pilaf, Almond, 74
Rice Stuffing, Wild, 72
Rice, Beans and Cheese
  Casserole, 93
Rice, Con Queso, 97
Ricotta Cream Cheese Spread, 135
Ricotta Frosting, Carob; 135
Roasted Almond Cookies, 128
Salad with Miso Dressing, Sprout,
  40
Salad with Yogurt Dressing,
  Mixed Grain, 43
Salad, California, 47
Salad, Italian Pasta, 48
Salad, Mock Chicken, 44
Salad, Rainbow Pasta, 48
Salad, Sunflower Potato, 41
Salad, Tempeh, 42
Salad, Waldorf, 46
San Bartelemao Bake, 108
Sandwich, Main Meal, 32
Sauce, Cranberry, 61
Sauce, Fig, 62
Sauce, Fruit, 62
Sauce, Green, 59
Sauce, Hearty Tomato, 58
Sauce, Italian Tomato, 58
Sauce, Miso-Pesto, 60
Sauce, Miso-Tahini, 60
Sauce, Mushroom, 58
Sauce, Orange Sesame, 60
Sauce, Summer Tomato Basil
  Sauce, 59
Sauce, Sweet Potato, 61
Sauce, Tofu, 35
Saucy Black Beans, 98
Sea salt, 11
Sea Vegetable Soup, Land &, 53
Sea vegetables, 11
Seasoning mix, 11
Sesame Sauce, Orange, 60
Shake, Papaya-Carob Malt, 137
Shake, Protein, 137
Shepherd's Pie, Macro, 103
Shitake mushrooms, 11
Slaw, Daikon, 40
Sloppy Joes, 89
Smoothie, Banana Date Nut, 136

Smoothie, Carob-Peanut Butter, 137
Smoothie, Tropical, 136
Smoothie, Yogurt, 136
Soup, Carrot-Yogurt, 56
Soup, Cool Avocado, 50
Soup, Curried Split Pea, 51
Soup, Fruit, 51
Soup, Humble Miso, 52
Soup, Land & Sea Vegetable, 53
Soup, Miso Wakame, 52
Soup, Mushroom-Barley, 55
Soup, Pumpkin, 54
Soup, Spicy Pea, 51
Soup, Spicy Tomato-Peanut, 54
Soup, Zucchini Yogurt, 50
Sour Cream, Lo-Cal Mock, 59
Spicy Pea Soup, 51
Spicy Tomato-Peanut Soup, 54
Spinach, Creamed, 68
Spinach-Tempeh Quiche, 90
Split Pea Soup, Curried, 51
Spread, Ricotta Cream Cheese, 135
Sprout Salad with Miso Dressing, 40
Sprouting, 16
Squares, Apricot, 124
Squash, Stuffed Butternut, 67
Stewed Plums, Rice Cereal with, 22
Strawberry Flip, 137
Stroganoff, Mushroom-Tofu, 79
Stuffed Butternut Squash, 67
Stuffed Cabbage Rolls with
   Butternut Sauce, 106
Stuffed Tofu Cutlets with
   Mushroom Sauce, 86
Stuffed Tofu in Green Sauce, 84
Stuffing, Apple-Date, 75
Stuffing, Cornbread, 72
Stuffing, Fruited Cous-Cous, 73
Stuffing, Wild Rice, 72
Summer Tomato Basil Sauce, 59
Sunflower Potato Salad, 41
Sushi, Vegetarian, 38
Sweet Potato Sauce, 61
Sweeteners, 14
Tahini, 11
Tahini Sauce, Miso; 60
Tamari, 11
Tartlettes, Carob Mousse, 124
Tea Muffins, 24
Tempeh, 11
Tempeh Almond Pate, 36
Tempeh Quiche, Spinach; 90
Tempeh Salad, 42
Tempeh with Indonesian
   Peanut Sauce, 91
Tempeh Wrap, Curried, 92
Tofu, 11, 15

Tofu Burgers, 78
Tofu Cornbread, Herbed, 27
Tofu Cutlets with Mushroom Sauce,
   Stuffed, 86
Tofu Dip or Sauce, 35
Tofu Fruit Whip, 130
Tofu in Green Sauce, Stuffed, 84
Tofu Loaf, 78
Tofu Mayonnaise, 40
Tofu Nut Loaf, 80
Tofu Nut Puree, 37
Tofu Stroganoff, Mushroom; 79
Tofu with Spicy Peanut Sauce,
   Marinated, 87
Tofu, Grilled, 78
Tofu-Lava, 127
Tomato Basil Sauce, Summer, 59
Tomato Sauce, Hearty, 58
Tomato Sauce, Italian, 58
Tomato-Peanut Soup, Spicy, 54
Topping, Whipped, 133
Tostada, Bean, 31
Trifle, Lemon Mousse, 113
Triticale, 11
Tropical Smoothie, 136
Tsimmes, 68
Tuna, Mock, 45
TVP, 11
Unclassical Reuben, 31
Vegetable Pate, 36
Vegetable Soup, Land & Sea, 53
Vegetable stock, 15
Vegetables, Indian Rice and, 101
Vegetarian Lasagne, 81
Vegetarian Sushi, 38
Vegie Ragout, Millet; 106
Wakame, 11
Wakame Soup, Miso, 52
Waldorf Salad, 46
Wehani rice, 11
Wheat Cakes, Blueberry, 21
Wheat Cakes, Buttermilk, 21
Whip, Desert, 129
Whip, Tofu Fruit, 130
Whipped Cream, Almond, 133
Whipped Topping, 133
Whole Wheat Chapatis, 28
Whole Wheat Drop Biscuits, 24
Wild Rice Stuffing, 72
Yogurt Cheese, Herbed, 35
Yogurt Cheesecake, Carob; 117
Yogurt Dressing, Mixed Grain
   Salad with, 43
Yogurt Smoothie, 136
Yogurt Soup, Carrot; 56
Yogurt Soup, Zucchini, 50
Zucchini Bread, 26
Zucchini Yogurt Soup, 50

about the authors

delia quigley

Delia Quigley presently lives in Siesta Key, Florida teaching yoga, studying macrobiotics and cooking gourmet vegetarian meals for private clients and friends.

This book is a compilation of recipes created during the two and a half years that Delia was the general manager of the deli kitchens for The Granary Inc., one of the largest natural foods companies in the southeastern United States. During this time she ran the kitchen facilities, staged live food demonstrations, co-hosted a weekly television show, "The Granary Gourmet", and taught evening cooking classes.

Delia has a BA degree in Theatre Arts from the University of Tampa and over the past twelve years has worked professionally as a director, writer, choreographer and performer while traveling extensively in Europe and the United States.

polly pitchford

Polly Pitchford switched from theater to the culinary arts when a vegetarian cooking class sparked an avid interest in natural foods. In 1984 she started working for The Granary, Inc. as assistant manager of the deli kitchens and co-hosted The Granary Gourmet television show.

At present Polly teaches aerobic classes and cooks macrobiotic meals privately for a small clientel. She lives in Sarasota with her husband, David, and continues her studies of nutrition and macrobiotics.

Order these titles directly
from Book Publishing Company:

Builders of the Dawn $17.95
Cooperative Method
    of Natural Birth Control $5.95
Dream Feather $9.95
George Bernard Shaw Vegetarian Cookbook . . . $8.95
Guide to Natural Foods Restaurants $9.95
How Can One Sell the Air? $4.95
Judy Brown's Guide
    to Natural Foods Cooking $10.95
Kids Can Cook $9.95
Murrieta Hot Springs Vegetarian Cookbook . . . $9.95
New Farm Vegetarian Cookbook $7.95
No Immediate Danger $11.95
Power of Your Plate $10.95
Shepherd's Purse:
    Organic Pest Control Handbook $6.95
Song of Seven Herbs $10.95
Spirit of the White Bison $5.95
Spiritual Midwifery; third edition $16.95
Starting Over:
    Learning to Cook with Natural Foods $10.95
Tempeh Cookbook $8.95
Ten Talents $16.95
this season's people $5.95
Tofu Cookery, revised $14.95
Tofu Quick & Easy $5.95
Vegetarian Cookbook for Diabetics $9.95

To order, please include $1 per book for postage and
handling.

Mail your order to:
    Book Publishing Company
    PO Box 99
    Summertown, TN 38483